Searching For My Sparkle

You Have Within You the Strength to Overcome Any Obstacle Life Throws at You

Coach Kelly S. MAEd., BSW

First published by Ultimate World Publishing 2023
Copyright © 2023 Kelly S. MAEd., BSW

ISBN

Paperback: 978-1-922982-01-8
Ebook: 978-1-922982-02-5

Kelly S. MAEd., BSW has asserted her rights under the Copyright, Designs and Patents Act 1988 to be identified as the author of this work. The information in this book is based on the author's experiences and opinions. The publisher specifically disclaims responsibility for any adverse consequences which may result from use of the information contained herein. Permission to use information has been sought by the author. Any breaches will be rectified in further editions of the book.

All rights reserved. No part of this publication may be reproduced, stored in or introduced into a retrieval system, or transmitted in any form, or by any means (electronic, mechanical, photocopying, recording or otherwise) without the prior written permission of the author. Any person who does any unauthorized act in relation to this publication may be liable to criminal prosecution and civil claims for damages. Enquiries should be made through the publisher.

Cover design: Ultimate World Publishing
Layout and typesetting: Ultimate World Publishing
Editor: Maddie Johnson

Ultimate World Publishing
Diamond Creek,
Victoria Australia 3089
www.writeabook.com.au

Dedication

To Mom and Dad:

For giving me life and a family to join. For working as hard as you did every day to provide for the children in your life of which I was one but didn't appreciate growing up. Please accept my heartfelt apology.

You may not know this right now, especially after reading this book I printed out in large print for you, but I do love you. I didn't appreciate everything you did for us growing up and I am sorry for that too, but now as an educated adult I understand you always worked hard and did the very best you knew how to do. Without you two, there would be no me to grow strong through all of life's obstacles and I thank you for teaching me all of that too.

To my Sonshine and Angels:

For changing my life in the most amazing way and giving me strength I didn't know I had.

You all taught me so many lessons every day, and I am still learning even after you began your own life journeys without me. I will always love you more.

To John:

For giving me the time and space to write this book and for keeping our refrigerator well-stocked, the floors vacuumed and washed, and for continuing to be the caring, loving man I've come to know and love during this chapter in my life.

I know you always say I don't have to thank you, but I really do want you to know how much you are truly appreciated, sweetheart.

Contents

Dedication	iii
Introduction	1
Chapter One: A Diamond is Born	7
Chapter Two: Beginning My Search for Love	19
Chapter Three: Mountains and Valleys	29
Chapter Four: A Tough Time for Christopher	39
Chapter Five: A Sparkle is Born	45
Chapter Six: From the Frying Pan into the Fire	55
Chapter Seven: M.S.? What's that?	65

Chapter Eight: Diamond When I Die	83
Chapter Nine: Moving on UP!	91
Chapter Ten: Two Steps Forward, One Step Back	101
Chapter Eleven: Starting to Polish	111
Chapter Twelve: Polishing Up the Diamond I Was Born to Be	121
My Final Letter	133
About The Author	137
Testimonials	139
Reflections	

Introduction

THIS BOOK IS WRITTEN FROM my point of view. The people in its pages are real, but if you ask any one of them, they will likely each have a different story. This is only how I see my life, not particularly exactly what happened from everyone's point of view. I skip over a lot of things that may have happened in my childhood, because I honestly don't remember a whole lot before my parents started taking in foster children. I don't remember the Social Worker who placed the foster children in our house ever asking us kids how we felt about sharing our childhood with others from outside the family. I probably wouldn't have minded until after my older sisters got married quite young and moved out of the house.

I wrote this book to see if I could figure out why my life turned out the way it did. Why do I get depressed so often and for so very long? Is it nature or nurture that comes from being raised by a woman who absolutely refused antidepressants when they were prescribed to her? I don't want to blame my mother for everything that has gone wrong in my life. In fact, I found my own way out of so many things and that could be because of the strength I learned from her, or from both my parents. I can even say that my ex-husband could be responsible for me going back to university and achieving my bachelor's and my master's as an adult. Being diagnosed with Multiple Sclerosis may be the reason I got out of a marriage I should have known better than to agree to in the first place.

I am sure my children leaving me alone for this chapter of my life has taught me lessons, too. I just haven't figured out yet what they may be. Just recently, my son and four of his kids got hit by a deer an hour away from where we live and he called me to come and help him out. I don't usually drive in the dark and my spouse, John, didn't really want me to go, but I told him he would go if it were his son and grandkids, so I am going. John's friend said to make sure the grandkids are there and it isn't some kind of a set-up. It wasn't, they were there, and I brought them home to spend the night before their ride came to pick them up the next morning. I finally got to meet my one-year-old granddaughter!

After I medically retired from my government position, I slept a lot. I started to feel like my life was wasting away, so I volunteered at two or three different places, began writing my life story, and had a reason to get out of bed every single morning — until Covid 19 hit and the world shut down. I thought maybe God was trying to tell me to slow down, and I started apologizing to everyone for the inconvenience that the virus outbreak had on everyone in so very many ways.

I have always liked to hear or read true life stories, or stories of celebrities, or anyone willing to share. I joined support groups online for people with MS, as well as for parents who were abandoned by their adult children. The people in my MS support groups said Covid 19 didn't change much for people with MS because they don't really go out anywhere, and especially not somewhere that doesn't have a toilet nearby. I agreed and I was glad I had the people from both support groups because nobody truly understands what I go through unless they've been there themselves.

So very many times I thought of committing suicide. I thought of running away from home when

I was three years old, and I did run away many times when I was 15. Also when I was 15, I took up smoking because I wanted to commit suicide, but I was too chicken to settle on which way to end my life. Then I went into foster care until the day I turned 16, when I dropped out of school, left the foster home in which I was living and moved in with my boyfriend. I thought of suicide again when I found out I was pregnant, twice, because I wasn't married, then again after I was diagnosed with MS. The answers always came from somewhere. I thought if I wrote this book, I might be able to finally figure out where they came from.

Over the course of my life, especially after I was thrown out of our marital home, I went through so much that a counsellor once told me the more pressure I felt, the more like a diamond I became. Diamonds are made from pressurized coal underground. A coach I met in my coaching classes told me I was born a diamond; I was just treated like coal for so long that I started treating myself like coal. That's when I started polishing off the coal and allowing my sparkle to shine through. Now, almost 27 years later, I coach other people with Multiple Sclerosis, or any other long-term disability, and help them to get their life back or design a new one. I went for a 2km walk with my mother and she mentioned how proud of me she was. She sees others with MS in nursing homes and even her next-door neighbour hardly comes outside, yet here I am walking with my 89-year-old mother and asking her to slow down! I'm proud of her, too! And that's probably where I get my strength.

> I'm a mother, I've been a wife, I have a life partner, and I've finally completed my education. Going through all of that taught me a lot. I will never give up, lay down and sleep my retirement away. Even a diagnosis of Multiple Sclerosis can't keep me down, due in part, I believe, to the strength I learned from my parents! Thanks Mom and Dad!

Chapter One

A Diamond is Born

WEDNESDAY, DECEMBER 15, 1965, IN a small city in Saskatchewan, a baby girl was born to a couple who already had two girls who were about to turn seven and nine. The family really wanted a boy, so nine months later they were expecting again and nine months after that, they finally had their boy! This story is about me, the third girl and the youngest 'big' sister. At my wedding, my eldest sister gave a toast to the bride and 'joked' about how 'happy' Dad was when he was told they had *another* baby girl when I was born. I was also told many times that not only was I born two weeks late, but I was the biggest baby in the hospital...like it was my fault.

My father owned a garage at the edge of the small village where we lived and my mother stayed home and took in boarders: usually teachers who were teaching at the school across the street from our house. Both of my parents were children of farmers, Dad was the eldest in his family so when he left High School he started working. His younger brothers went on to university and achieved their master's and one even became a professor, while the youngest brother stayed on and took over the family farm. My Mother was the second of a set of twins born so tiny the midwife told her father that she probably won't live, but she sure showed them! They had a sister ten years older and a sister ten years younger and a bunch of brothers sprinkled in there too. So to help out with the family finances, my Mother dropped out of school after she completed Grade 8.

She started waitressing and met this tall handsome mechanic and married him! Together they moved to a village close to his parent's farm, bought a house and started a family. Dad was very busy in his garage and Mother kept herself busy doing laundry, cooking, cleaning and looking after a pig they kept in a pen in the woods across the street. There was a huge garden on the property, so besides cooking meals for her family and boarders, she also got into canning and freezing fruits and vegetables — on top of every other chore that needed to be done while raising children. My parents were very busy adults, far too busy to sit on the floor with their children and ever play with us. They even took in foster children to help parents who needed it, which made the portion of individual time spent with each of their children even smaller than it already was.

I remember going to visit my mother's parents almost every weekend as a child. My maternal grandparents spoke very little English, or I only remember them speaking Ukrainian around me. It wasn't even until years later when my eldest sister's boyfriend (and eventual husband) stopped in at our grandparent's place to drop something off that she spoke English to him! I had trouble believing him when he told me she speaks perfectly understandable English, because she had never spoken one English word to me that I could remember.

Another thing I remember as a child was walking along the woods across the street from our house, where mother could still see me if she looked out the window. I knew she wouldn't like to know the thoughts going through my head. I wondered what would happen to me if I ran away from home. I didn't because I knew nobody in their right mind would pick up someone so small who is running away from home. They would bring me back to the house and I would be in big trouble. I really don't remember a whole lot about my childhood, and I have always thought that's because my mind won't allow me to remember difficult memories.

Both my Ukrainian/Polish parents had decided when they had children that they would teach us English first, which was smart because it was the official language in Canada. My mother mentioned that when she was in school, when Ukrainian-speaking children spoke to each other in their native language, they would get smacked on their fingers with a ruler. Many teachers at that time didn't understand Ukrainian, and First Nation children were also getting swats over their fingers for talking in their native language. Besides, I also believed my parents wanted to talk about their children in front of us without us being able to understand them. I came to that conclusion after they wouldn't allow me to take Ukrainian as a second language in Grade 7, even though that was one of the choices and that's the second language I originally wanted to learn. They said French was the second official Canadian language and learning it would help me get a job, which in the end it never did.

Before their younger two children started kindergarten, my parents decided to move to

The house we lived in when I was born

The church we attended was at the end of our backyard

a bigger city to get a better education for their children. Dad was also being too kind with his neighbours and friends by giving them such a good deal and letting them charge it when he fixed their vehicles. He knew from growing up on a farm that farmers only get paid once a year when they sell their grain. So my parents figured out a way to get a mortgage and build a house of their own to raise their family in Yorkton. The older two girls boarded with friends and were able to move to Yorkton and start school before the house was finished being built. Dad put the garage up for sale but stayed working there until the bungalow was finished in a relatively newer area of the city. He then was hired as a mechanic in Yorkton so the family could finally live all under one roof in our new home.

I started Kindergarten in Yorkton in a little church right beside the elementary school I would be enrolled in the following year. I LOVED going to school and getting away from home. I would get a ride to and from school every day until one day I couldn't see the car, so I just walked home. Soon after that Mom wasn't as worried about me walking to and from school. I had the best teacher EVER in Grade 1. Mrs. Donna Whitta was so very, very nice to me I clung onto everything she said every day. I cried when Grade 1 was over, but my Grade 2 teacher, Mrs. Hudema, was absolutely fabulous as well. I will never forget her teaching me how to spell the word 'people' by sounding it out – Pee-o-pl-e! She also wanted me to send her a copy of the first book I publish, and I do plan to! Mother found a job in a daycare the year my little brother started kindergarten, two years after me.

It was shortly after that when a couple kids came to live with us and we were told their names were Bonnie and Wayne. Actually, the girl's name was Karen, but we already had a Karen in the house (my eldest sister) so we were told she chose the name Bonnie. Bonnie was a few months younger than me, but a year behind me in school. Wayne was a couple years older and a year ahead. My older sisters stayed with us and helped us get ready after our parents went to work about ninety minutes before we had to leave for school.

I made many friends in school and many were talking about sleeping over at each other's houses, so I wanted to get in on it too. I had a 'BFF' before those letters became commonplace and she lived at the edge of the city, but she didn't know her address. I didn't ask my parents if I could, but I invited Kara over to spend the night one weeknight. Mom blew up when we walked through the door and asked, "Who's this?" I said, "Kara's come to spend the night!" Mom absolutely refused to accept this and wanted Dad to drive her home. Kara didn't know what her address was because she lived in one of Yorkton's first 'suburbs,' and she ended up spending the night. I was never going to do that again, I was soooo embarrassed! The next year Kara didn't even come back to the same school, and I thought it was because she didn't like me. I held onto that thought for years...

Dad was a hard-working mechanic and I thought our family was financially comfortable, even though they would complain about being so broke all the time and how they gave up so many things to have four children and look after foster kids as well. I even told one of my band teachers one day that I probably wouldn't be able to go on a trip that was being planned to play in a band festival because my parents had been complaining about how much money it was going to cost them. They got very upset with me for saying that to anyone after the teacher offered them alternative ways to pay for the trip. I guess they didn't want people to think they were broke and they would never accept charity.

Karen was nine years older than me, so she graduated Grade 12 and started university in a different, bigger city. For about a year, my other Sister Connie had to stay with all the younger children so our parents wouldn't be late for work. I don't recall who told us first, but Connie became pregnant at 16, and 18-year-old Karen eloped with her High School sweetheart in Saskatoon. They both got married the same year. When Karen came home from university for a weekend, her new husband, Garth, came with her and they slept in the same bed. I knew Mom and Dad never would have allowed that, so I had to ask Karen why, and that was when I was informed they were married. I heard a lot of yelling and screaming about parents having to sign forms before their 16-year-old daughter could get married in the Catholic Church, even if she was pregnant. I remember Connie's husband saying to me as he walked out of the church after marrying my older sister that he should have waited five years and married me! It was tough trying to fall asleep through all of the arguing, but after Connie moved in with her husband things got even worse for me.

Now that Wayne was the oldest in the house, he was in charge after the parents went to work. I had a friend who lived a couple of blocks away, so I would either try to get a ride with them or walk to school. Wayne would chase me around the house most mornings so he could pull my pants and panties down and check on the growth of my pubic hair. This went on for about four years until he turned 16 and wanted to move out on his own. I didn't tell my parents about how he was treating me because I thought they had been through so much with both their daughters getting married in the same year. Plus, I didn't think they would believe their 'precious foster child' would be capable of something like that, and their older daughters lied and got married early, so why would I be any different? Mother had become so visibly depressed that her doctor prescribed anti-depressants for her. She refused to take them saying she would 'work it out on her own' but I felt she was just taking it out on us kids.

Rachel started attending our school when we were in Grade 5. She would sit alone at lunch, so one day I sat beside her and we became fast friends. Her family moved to a house a couple blocks from us so we started walking home from school together. She had to walk a couple of blocks further than me, but she would always walk me from school to my door. While walking home together, we found we had a lot in common. She had older sisters too, but she also had two brothers: one older and one younger than her. She invited everyone in the class over for her birthday party, so I was allowed to go too. At the party, she decided to have her friends spend the night, but because it was a school night, I was not allowed to stay overnight at her place. I was the one and only person from that party who had to walk home before dark. And I was sad again...

My pre-teen years were absolutely horrific, getting up before school at 6am so my parents could be at work by 7am and by 7:30am, being chased around the house by my foster 'brother' while he was supposed to be in charge after my parents left for work, and not even being able to talk about things with my older sisters who had married and moved on with their lives without me. There were times when I would 'sneak' over to my sister Connie's place after she gave birth to Cameron. I remember one time I did a cartwheel in their living room and little Cameron was so entertained he let out his first real belly laugh. Oh, how I loved that little boy, and his tiny little sister born two years later who was so small her nickname was 'mouse.' A few years later Cameron would tease his little sister saying when she grew up she would be a rat! She sure showed him though. While studying Business Administration in university, she modelled and had some pictures published in a magazine. She sure turned into one gorgeous, sweet little rat!

I did see Mrs. Whitta many years later when I was working at the Credit Union and I didn't recognize her face, but as soon as I saw her name on her paperwork I knew who she was. I was wearing a name tag with only my first name on it and she asked me if my last name was Protz. I think I said to her, "Seriously? How did you know after all the students you must have taught?" She said back to me "Oh, your eyes haven't changed." I still get all choked up even just telling this story. Grades 1 & 2 were by far my best years in school, until I started University of course.

> During my early years I guess I could say I learned to walk on eggshells and watch my words when speaking around or near either one of my parents. I didn't like to hear them yell and my sisters had already put them both through so much, I didn't want to do the same. After becoming an adult I learned to understand how they were raised differently and how changing their parenting style must have been very difficult to do while raising their own children. They just raised their children like they were raised. None of their siblings eloped or got pregnant at 16, so my parents didn't know how to raise the rest of us after their oldest daughters devastated them like that.

Chapter Two

Beginning My Search for Love

Wʜᴇɴ ᴘᴇᴏᴘʟᴇ sᴛᴀʀᴛ ᴛᴏ ғᴇᴇʟ neglected, ignored and not good enough from a very young age, all kinds of different things happen for and to them over the course of their life. Growing up, I was never once told "I love you" by either one of the people who brought me into this world. They said their parents never told them that, but they 'always knew.' It wasn't the same for me. What I knew was I had two older sisters who hardly ever came back to visit, I had a foster 'sister' who was constantly praised by my parents, and I even remember coming home from a final Band Concert one school year and we all got into trouble for not receiving any awards! Yes, Karen and Connie were really good in band and would always receive awards at their final concerts. Now that they weren't there...and the band director 'forgot' my scholarship to band camp for the summer when everyone else got theirs, none of us were called up to the stage that night. I did get the scholarship a few days later but by then, it was too late, and there was no apology forthcoming.

I started babysitting for neighbours and teachers from the school when I was 12. I would babysit every chance I got. I loved to clean, play with the kids, and I shouldered the responsibility well. Plus, I would get paid a whole dollar for every hour I would spend at their house! A dollar an hour was good pay at that age, a package of cigarettes only cost a dollar or maybe just a few cents more. Babysitting would get me out of the house where there was always so much tension it was like I could slice through it with a knife. Life was just easier when I babysat, ran away from home, or just got out of the house for any reason at all... like band camp.

I joined band in Grade 5, as early as I could. I wanted to play the piano, but Mom said they couldn't afford to buy a piano for me to practice on, so I settled for playing the flute. I absolutely loved making music and wanted to learn everything as quickly as possible. That first year I practiced so often that along with one other student, we were invited into a 'special' class of our own. One time the band teacher asked us both to hold a note as long as possible. I held the note longer than he did and he was playing a trombone into which he blew all the air from his mouth. The teacher said he should have been able to hold the note longer because I was blowing air across the hole to play the flute. That first year at the band festival I didn't know I was the only person in my age group, so I won first place! In Junior High School there were two bands, A and B bands. The B band was mostly for students in grades 7 and 8, but the A band was for the best players in grades 8 and 9. I played with the B band in Grade 6 and the A band in grades 7-9. I usually sat very close to first chair.

The A band would get together to practice at the High School early in the mornings before school started, then a bus would take us to our school as soon as band practice was over. I didn't mind going into school early because it meant I wouldn't be chased around the house that morning and my Dad would drop me off at the High School on his way to work. Band practice days were a great reason to get up early in the morning. I did so

21

well that I was invited to join the jazz band, which didn't have flutes, but the fingerings were the same on the saxophone, so they asked me if I wanted to play the sax with the jazz band. I said I would, so band practices, performances and trips were the highlight of Junior High School years for me.

Well that, along with the trip the school arranged for the second language students to go to the countries where the second languages they were studying originated. By this time Kara and I were at the same school together, and we went on that trip together, but we had already made other friends. We needed to do lots of fundraising for that trip because the student's parents couldn't afford to pay for it all. Mine did pay for a lot, and they not only sent me but my foster 'brother' as well. Yes, the guy that would chase me around the house after my parents left for work most mornings. They didn't know that was going on, and they didn't want to be accused of treating their own children better than the foster kids. The entire trip was well supervised, so there was not much untoward that happened on that trip. I did spend a lot of time with my first ever 'boyfriend.' I was really hurt when we got home and I never heard from him again until after I was already seeing someone else. He said now that your parents are allowing you to date, maybe we should get together? My parents never actually 'allowed' me to date, I had to see guys behind their back, probably because of how my two older sisters left the house.

I had to share my room with the girl we were told wanted to be called Bonnie, and my younger brother had to share his bedroom with his foster 'brother.' There was a master suite and two bedrooms on the main floor, and Dad built a bedroom in the basement that was never legal, but where the oldest children in the house were allowed sleep. I say it wasn't legal because there were no windows in that room so if there was ever a fire in that house anyone sleeping in that room had no chance of getting out. When the oldest foster 'brother' stayed in that room he snuck out of the other basement windows at night and came back whenever he felt like it. The day he turned 16 he left foster care, went to jail for a while and lifted weights, getting huge muscles. My younger brother made new friends at school and when they were at the mall one Thursday he saw his foster 'brother' in the distance. He yelled out at the top of his lungs "Hey ya big fucking Indian!" and both his friends turned around to walk in the other direction, one of them repeating "We're gonna die...we're gonna die!" They would laugh about that later.

When I started getting interested in boys if any one of them said "I love you" my knees would go weak and I would give him anything and everything he asked of me. I felt so privileged in Grade 9 when I met the cutest guy I had ever seen in my entire life, David, and he wanted to date me. ME! I had trouble believing it! He didn't ask my parent's permission, but by that time both my sisters were married and to my mother, all boys were evil in her mind, and she would never allow me to date. He had a car and would drive the route from my Junior High to my home so he could pick me up and give me a ride home. The first time we met was at the High School one morning before band. He was visiting with friends he knew at that High School because he attended the Catholic High School. I had no idea who this guy was, but he sure looked like all that and a bag of chips, with his gorgeous blonde hair and hypnotizing blue eyes. He was the first guy I kissed with my mouth open, in fact before him I didn't even realize people did kiss with their mouths open.

In December, all the girls from my class wanted to get together for a meal after school one evening. I told them my Mom probably wouldn't allow me to go, but they told me to ask anyway. They were planning it close to my birthday, so they suggested I tell her they wanted to take me out for my birthday. I explained that to my parents, but they absolutely would not allow it. I had all kinds of female friends in Grade 9 until I started High School the following year. I never once had a birthday party when I was growing up, I was lucky if I might have one friend over to play while their mother visited with my mother. Not many people want to celebrate a birthday ten days before Christmas, they're usually too busy going to Christmas parties and broke spending money on Christmas presents. I'd be heartbroken every year.

Then a few months before Grade 9 ended, we had to apply for the different classes we wanted to take in High School, which precipitated the first time I ran away from home. I wanted to include typing and accounting in the classes I chose and Mother wanted me to take French (because they paid for my trip to Paris and Germany in Grade 8) and Christian Ethics. She told Dad to deal with it and left for work. Dad 'dealt with it' by breaking a quarter inch thick board over my hand before dropping me off at the High School for band in the morning. My friend found me crying in the bathroom before band and decided to walk with me to our school. I talked to the principal about my hand and he asked if I wanted to go to the hospital and have it looked at, he would call my father to pick me up and drive me there. I said "No, please don't call my father!" He did anyway and Dad yelled at me all the way to the hospital for taking him away from his work, threw a quarter at me and told me to call him for a ride back to school when I was done. I walked back to school because it wasn't that far and I didn't want to be yelled at again. After school I went to my friend's and phoned my mother to tell her what had happened that morning and that I was scared to come home, so I was going to stay the night with a friend. She said if I tried to do that she would call the police and have me picked up, brought home and my friend's parents would be in trouble. Because I didn't want to get anyone else in trouble, I decided to go home and take my consequences like I was getting used to.

I was asked to attend David's Grade 12 graduation. He had to pick me up from home and drop me off by midnight, but since he was three years older than me, he had friends to hang out with after the prom. I didn't know any of them and thought I would probably feel really out of place, so I bought a blue gown and attended his graduation with him. He did end up dropping me off before midnight and went out to the after-grad parties that I heard all about. He was then going away to be a counsellor at a cadet camp he had attended when he was younger and decided to break up with me before he left. We got back together later that summer and I went with his parents to drop him off at the Bus Depot when he joined the army that fall. I cried but had been introduced to many of his friends who I did spend time with when he was gone.

Many of his friends were kids who skipped classes, smoked cigarettes and marijuana, drank alcohol, experimented with other drugs, met for coffee and spent weekends together. I heard from them that some female students who attended the Catholic High School with David wanted him to ask them to go to the prom with him, but instead he asked me. They concluded I must be sleeping with him and that's why he asked me and not them. I decided the next time he was home on a leave from the army I was going to sleep with him for the first time. Why not? So many people thought I already did, so I may as well…right? Besides, I was already 15-years-old!

After giving birth to my own daughters I realize now that 15 is far too young to become an adult. My son started smoking and both my daughters felt grown up, but that's not how I saw them. I do wish now in some ways that I would have stayed a child when I was a child, but I learned a lot from 'doing things my way' too.

Chapter Three

Mountains and Valleys

I MADE A FRIEND WHO shared the same first name as me and who lived nearby. We used to meet at the park across from her house just down the street from where we lived. We had just started to become close friends when her parents decided to pack up and move. I wanted to share this milestone in my life, so I wrote her a letter all about my first time, and then I ran away from home to see David one night. He convinced me to go home (and to never sleep with anyone who wouldn't use a condom) and he walked into the house with me. I hadn't told him about writing that letter and what it said, but my parents called me a slut and a whore before they told him they had just read my letter about having sex with him. He tried to calm them down by saying we only did it once and they said they read we had done it multiple times. I interrupted them and told them I was exaggerating, but they were looking at me now just like they had looked at Connie when she got pregnant at 16. David and I broke up shortly after that happened.

I was walking home from school with Rachel one day and a white Camaro stopped and asked us if we wanted a ride home. We both didn't know the driver but recognized a couple of the guys in the car so we said "OK!" Rachel sat in the front right beside the driver and I sat in the back when they all introduced us to the driver – Chris. He was three years older than us and was working full-time at a Stereo store installing car stereos in vehicles. I liked Chris from the day we met, but Rachel was not only gorgeous (with much bigger boobs) and fun to be with, but she sat in the front seat so she and Chris started dating. They made a great couple and I didn't think I had a chance with him anyway, so we just became good friends. Like any and every teenager I knew, I wanted to hang out with my friends, go out for coffee, and cruise up and down Broadway Street while listening to loud music. When Chris would drop me off before taking Rachel home, my parents would always comment about how loud and annoying the music was coming from his Camaro. He used to come to the high school and pick up whoever wanted to go cruise with him at lunch time while everyone was on a break. I would always be willing to go cruising with Chris at lunch time in his Camaro.

I ran away from home many times after that, because when I was out from under their roof and under their control I finally felt 'normal,' like every other student at school. After running away, I actually went out on dates and got to know so many people. Before that I was hanging around with kids who skipped school, drank, did drugs and smoked cigarettes. I dated David's younger brother Stephen for a bit and became really good friends with his sister Karen who was my age. I was also able to get along and hang out with all kinds of different people, and I could never understand why those girls who were friends with me in Grade 9 didn't want to hang out with me any more in High School. But I met a whole new group of people who accepted me as I was. Karen was going to the Catholic High School so when she found out she was pregnant she went to a group home in Regina for unwed mothers and made arrangements for her baby to be adopted.

I finished Grade 10 and passed every class except for Social Studies, which I took in second semester. So I enrolled in all Grade 11 classes with the students I had been going to school with for so many years, and only had to take one class with the students who were a year behind us. Then came the awful news that Rachel's parents were getting divorced because her father had been cheating on her Mother even while building a huge new home for his family in a newer area of the city. They decided to send Rachel away to a boarding school that was connected to their church, so she was no longer going to High School with me and I was very sad about that, but I did have other friends, and Chris was still driving to High School at noon to cruise around with friends and I was still one of them.

It was around this time my sister Connie decided to move to Regina so she could take nursing because that was one thing she could get into having only completed Grade 11. She took both her children with her and filed for a divorce from her husband. She told us he was abusive to her and she wanted to get her children away from that horrible life. She did all this on her own because mother and father had hardly spoken with her since she left and married her husband. Connie had met her husband through some church activity of some kind, so nothing I was invited to was ever 'safe' enough for me to attend. In fact, I didn't even drink coffee so Mother wouldn't let me go out for 'coffee' with friends until I started, so I did. Dad drank coffee with seven teaspoons of sugar, and it didn't taste all that bad.

Things at school were going alright, but at home I felt more and more unwanted, unneeded, and overlooked. I spent more time with my friends and when my parents said no I ran away from home and went out anyway. I didn't get into any legal trouble, but my parents already 'lost' their older daughters and wanted to hold on tighter to me and not allow me to go anywhere or do anything. I had lost the one best friend I had who moved when her father was transferred to a different city, my other best friend went into a boarding school and the love of my life at this point was in the army, and even after his dishonourable discharge he rarely ever came back to Yorkton. One time I ran away, the police stopped a car I was in, asked me my name and I was honest. They said "we've been looking for you," and took me home. My parents had been in touch with social services and they had emergency workers come to the house and take me into foster care. The emergency workers heard the whole story and told the temporary foster 'mother' the circumstances and she treated me really well the entire time I lived in their house. She allowed me to go to a school dance I had been fighting with my parents about. Then they took me over to their 'friend's place' where I was sexually molested by some kid my age, but life had to go on.

I was moved into a group home for foster kids in Yorkton and decided that school wasn't paying me enough money to continue, so the day I turned 16, I dropped out of high school to find a job. Chris and I had stayed friends even though he and Rachel were dating long-distance, writing letters and talking on the phone. I didn't realize how much I felt for him until he told me Rachel had broken up with him over the phone and I had to look out the window because I couldn't help but smile. We started dating shortly after that and when I quit school, I moved out of the group home and right into Chris's apartment, which he shared with a few of his friends. I found a babysitting job and worked at other part-time jobs, like one at the roller skating rink.

Chris wasn't ready to tell his parents we were living together, so when his mom came to Yorkton and I went for coffee with her and his younger sister while Chris was at work, he asked me not to mention it. When his mom asked who all lives at the place where I was living, I didn't think about it and named off some of Chris's roommates. Chris' sister, Linda, later told me that I told their mom we were living together, and I said "no I didn't!" Linda explained when their mom asked how many people were living in the same place I was, she was curious to know how many foster kids were in the group home. When I started naming off Chris's friends, she knew. I hurried straight to Chris's workplace and apologized to him over and over again. I don't think Chris ever showed his anger to me once in the four years we dated off and on.

We did get our own place without his friends and traveled out to his parents' farm in Sheho for every Ukrainian Christmas and sometimes even for December 25, but they didn't really celebrate that day. I got to know and really admire his mom, we would play bingo together after she taught me how to keep up with the caller and bring little good luck charms to each game. His sister and younger brother and I got along really well too, and I admired his father for raising such wonderful kids. His older brother Steve didn't like me much and Steve's wife never had a nice thing to say about me, but Chris loved me and I loved him…and that was all that mattered to us.

My friend Karen had moved back to Yorkton from the group home for unwed mothers in Regina and was having difficulties in the Catholic High School because so many other female students knew she had a baby and would avoid her. She thought she should drop out like I did and move in with us. We told her that if she drops out of school we would be charging her a higher rent because she could get a job and afford it, but if she transferred over to the Public High School and finished her Grade 12 her rent would be minimal, so she decided to transfer and she did find other girls who had given birth and continued school to get at least their Grade 12. She wasn't avoided like the plague, so this High School drop-out was able to help one of my closest friends graduate, even though I wasn't ready to yet.

There was another girl I was spending time with who went with me one day to K-Mart because she wanted to show me how easy it was to shoplift. I thought I saw someone watching us, but after she picked up the make-up we were walking away and I told her to put it in my purse because it had a lot of room. Just as we were leaving the store some adults walked up to us and asked us to come with them. We asked why and they said someone saw my friend stealing and they wanted to see where the product was. Once we were in a separate room, I opened my purse and they said they had to charge me with possession of stolen items, but the person who saw the theft saw my friend steal, so off to court I went. I got a conditional discharge and met an absolutely fabulous probation officer who suggested we meet at A&W for coffee instead of me having to find a ride all the way across the city to her office. She was one of the first adults who talked to me like a human being. I wasn't used to that, it hadn't happened since my Grade 1 and 2 teachers. On the last day I met with my probation officer she even bought me a mug with my name on it. I really liked her.

Once Grade 11 was over Rachel moved back to Yorkton and we continued our friendship. She understood that Chris and I were in love, and she just wanted to spend time with me like she really couldn't when I was living with my parents. She came to our place late one evening and I let her in with a mutual friend of ours and our friend's boyfriend. Our place was the closest to where they had to walk from and Chris went back to bed to sleep while I stayed up and visited. All of them had just been kicked out of his older brother's car because Rachel was not interested in him. When there was a knock at the door even later that night we asked who it was and didn't get an answer. The guy that showed up with Rachel and her friend asked if it was his twin brother by name and the answer was a quiet 'yes' so we opened the door and it turned out to be his older brother with a sawed off shotgun with which he shot Rachel in the back of her head. He then pointed the gun at everyone else in the room while yelling and screaming profanities and left. Chris woke up and came out of our room to see how he could help. There was another knock at the door and we thought the guy with the gun was back, so we asked "who is it?" and didn't get an answer. Chris looked out the window and said he saw a police car outside, so we asked, "Is it the police?" They said "Yes it is." We opened the door for them.

> I guess I felt at the time that I couldn't learn anything from a lecture at home, I needed to make my own mistakes to learn my own lessons the 'hard' way. I just wish I wouldn't have hurt so many people in the process.

Chapter Four

A Tough Time for Christopher

THE NEXT DAY I COULDN'T stop crying while cleaning up blood from the carpet and waiting to hear from Rachel's mother at the hospital about how she was doing. The doctors told her they could do surgery and take the pellets out of her skull, but were afraid they may do more damage than good. Nobody wanted that, and Rachel could go on and use pharmaceuticals to deal with her pain. She went on to take a secretarial course and we stayed in touch after that for years. Years later she met and married a Romanian man and they had one son together...but that's a story for later on.

Chris and I would drive out to their acreage to visit and play cards with my sister Karen and her husband Garth who got along very well with Chris. In fact, everyone who knew Chris got along well with him, so it was no wonder that we stayed together from when I was about to turn 16 until after I turned 20, off and on. We kept breaking up because of my own insecurities and because I never really felt I had lived a 'teenage' life. The life I was living with Chris was a grown-up life, paying bills, cooking, cleaning and 'playing house.' We made a great couple, but I don't think I ever thought I was good enough for him, and that was probably true at that time.

I wasn't getting paid very much so I decided to move in with my sister in Regina and look for employment there. Chris was going to follow me as soon as he found work. It didn't take long at all for Chris to find work. My sister suggested he apply to work nights in the group home where she was working, so he moved to Regina. Soon his older brother moved to Regina to work in a different Stereo store and Chris got the job installing car stereos. I worked at the day care my niece and nephew attended to fill in every now and then. I worked part-time jobs in restaurants as a waitress or fast food at the till for a while.

Chris and I had broken up when I started working full-time at a gas station that had a carwash attached. I figured I should probably be able to afford to pay my own rent and stop living off Chris. We were still friendly and stayed in touch, but I was meeting new people all the time now and everyone I met up to this point was always very nice to me. I met this one fellow who drove a Harley Davidson motorcycle and wore black leather from head to toe. We did things like go for coffee and then the bar and parties when I didn't work at night. He never did try to kiss me, so I thought he only thought of me as a friend. We would go to parties and he would encourage me to get together with guys who were interested in me, so I just thought that was the kind of friendship we were going to have. It was too late when one of the girls who was dating a friend of his told me he had always wanted to be more than friends with me.

I met a couple of guys whose first names were Dave (go figure!). One of them was a red-headed university student and the other was a cab driver. The cab driver would stop by the gas station every night after his shift and one night he asked me out. He took me to this restaurant where each customer cooked their own steak to just the way they liked it, and it was a part of the racquetball court where he was a member. I don't remember whether or not I slept with him that first night, but I probably did because as soon as someone treated me nice and paid attention to me, I didn't want it to end. We started spending lots of time together and when the red-headed university student Dave stopped by the gas station one night and asked me out, I felt I had to say "no thank you."

The cab driver introduced me to his mother, sister, and his older brother, and we looked for an apartment to move into together. We found one just down the street from his parent's place and I put a deposit on it of $180.00, but for some reason we decided to take one closer to the middle of the city where I found work. I do remember getting that deposit back, but the cheque was made out to both of us so I couldn't cash it. He had me sign the back and took it into his bank and could only deposit it, so he couldn't give me the cash back that day…and he never did. We travelled to Yorkton together once with a tent, met Rachel and the boyfriend she ended up marrying, and camped in a tent in the city campground. We camped in another campground in a valley and he carved our initials into a tree trunk, but then one night he wanted to have sex and remembering what David had said to me, I said only with a condom. I kept saying "no" especially after the condom broke, but he kept going and got me pregnant that night.

Because Chris and I were still friends Dave asked me how I knew this was his baby, and I told him because I didn't sleep with anyone else. He asked me about Chris and I said we're friends, we don't still sleep together! He didn't believe me and probably told his mother the baby wasn't his because I called her and she didn't want to talk to me or make arrangements to see her grandchild after being born. I decided that since I was going to be a mother I didn't want to raise my child on Welfare, so I enrolled in a couple of correspondence High School classes and moved back in with my parents. Chris and I would still talk on the phone, and we stayed in touch even though my parents never wanted to meet him or get to know him at all, ever. They never did give him a chance - their loss.

One day my mother told me she had a dream that I gave birth and she was with me the whole time and that thought absolutely scared me sick. I didn't want to share the most important day of my life so far with a woman who cared more about her foster children, job and her depression than she did about me. My parents wouldn't even show up for a meeting with me and my Social Worker when I was in care because they heard I was still smoking and had too many friends. The Social Worker wrote up all kinds of lies in his reports about me being lazy, immature and a juvenile delinquent. The Probation Officer and the people I babysat for disagreed with him, but when I moved to Regina and in with my sister I applied to Social Services for welfare to pay my sister rent and they read over and believed the Social Worker from Yorkton's notes, and not me. Social Workers hadn't done me any good so far in my life. I didn't have to collect Welfare for long because I started working part-time at Burger Baron, and then full-time at MacDonald's before Chris moved to Regina.

After my mother told me about her dream, I was worried it might come true, so the next time I talked to Chris on the phone I asked him if I could move in with him again and he sounded delighted. I packed a bag and was on the next bus to Regina to live with Chris again. I brought all my school books with me and made arrangements to write the exams and I passed both classes with flying colours. Then I found an exam I could take as an adult that would get me my Grade 12 equivalence, so I studied, took it and passed that one too.

> I remember discussing with Connie too that I felt my parents seemed to need to 'control' me and I felt I needed to learn to control myself. Connie said that when I was living under their roof they did need to have some control. I pouted about that until my children turned that age, and I began to think the same way as Connie had.

Chapter Five

A Sparkle is Born

I STILL WASN'T SURE AT this time whether or not I was going to give the baby up for adoption, but mother said to me that if that was my decision, they would adopt the child. Looking back on my childhood I didn't dare even look into adoption because I didn't want my baby to have a childhood like I had. Of course, that was all I knew so I raised him exactly as I was raised while hoping all the time to do so much better than my parents did. I didn't have very much luck with Social Workers, so I didn't even think to call them and talk it over with an 'outside person' but as we lay in bed at night I would discuss it over and over with Chris. We even came up with a name together and I decided to honour his father by giving a boy, if that's what I had, the middle name of Jonathan (because Chris' Dad's name was John).

Chris stayed awake and with me the whole time I was in labour except when he had to be at work. I went into the hospital that first night in labour really early in the morning. He stayed until later that morning and when he had to leave for work the nurses told him it would still be a while because of how little I had dilated. He came back right after work and stayed awake until I gave birth to a baby boy on December 21, 1984, 6 days after my 19th birthday. We named him Kyle Jonathan Protz. Twenty-two hours of hard labour with quick naps in between until the contractions got too close together. I never dreamed it would ever be this difficult and I don't remember who told me that you forget the pain of delivery after the baby's born, but I couldn't forget. I decided then and there that I was never ever going to have another baby.

Connie had decided to move to Victoria when I was pregnant and two months after Kyle was born, she sent us a ticket to fly to Victoria to visit her and her kids. I flew with Kyle for the first time when he was only two months old, and being in Victoria meant we were closer to sea level, so Kyle started sleeping through the night at two months of age and kept sleeping through the night even after we flew home to Regina. Chris didn't come with us because he had to work, but I missed him like crazy while we were away. When we got back to Saskatchewan, we kept visiting his parent's farm and seeing his sister so I decided to ask Chris' sister Linda and my brother Clark to be Godparents and both said they would!

I was having difficulty being intimate with Chris and I wanted to be, so I decided to go and see a counsellor to see if I could figure out why. In discussion with the counsellor, she had me hold a mirror to my private parts and examine them, hoping to get me to like myself again. When I told her the circumstances under which I became pregnant, she said "oh, so you were raped." It wasn't a question, but I said I didn't think I was. Then she asked me if I ever once said "yes." And I had to be honest with her and tell her I didn't. But he wasn't hitting me or yelling at me or being angry with me, but she said, "you didn't say yes, so you were date raped." No wonder I was having difficulty being intimate with Chris.

Kyle was not even a year old when he had a febrile grand mal seizure and scared me half to death. Connie had moved back to Regina with her kids and was working in the hospital I took Kyle to. She walked into his room, saw me crying and told me to stop it! Kyle was going to wake up and seeing me cry would scare him and he wouldn't be able to stop crying. I learned not to cry in front of my children, which is a habit that would bite me in the ass in the future. We found out that my father had seizures as a child and grew out of them, and two of my oldest sister's kids did too, so he wasn't going to die on me, Thank God.

Chris worked during the day and said he would watch the baby in the evenings if I wanted to find a job where I would work in the evenings, so I started working at a bar on Broad Street. I would be with Kyle during the days and Chris would look after him in the evenings so I could work. Then I decided to stop putting Chris through all of this, so I moved back in with my parents and started going back to High School at the age of 20 and as a single parent. My parents wouldn't attend Kyle's baptism because they disagreed with my choice of Godparents, my brother and Chris' sister Linda. I took everyone out to a restaurant after church so mother wouldn't have to cook and clean up after the celebration. They were still refusing to meet Chris and give him a chance to prove his worth.

I was able to pay for the meal because after school I took a job at the Shopper's Drug Mart in the mall. I worked the till at the front of the store and was always at the mall where the students would hang out after school and in the evenings. I liked that job because I was able to learn how to work the till quite easily, and I got discounts on things I needed to buy for myself and for my son. I was allowed to use Dad's second car because Mother was working from home looking after other people's children while their parents would go off to work, or to school and work in my case. I was gone all day at school and most of the evenings I worked, so I left my son with family. Of course, the only reason I survived was because I started living on caffeine pills from Shopper's Drug Mart.

Some of the students at the High School made fun of me because of the way I dressed, but there were students who had been friends with my brother who went off to university the year before and they took me under their wing. They were all very nice to me while I took a full load of classes during the day and looked after my son and studied in the evenings. I wanted to get through Grade 12 as soon as possible, so I took more classes than I probably should have so I was asked for a deposit for graduation. I said I wasn't going. The president of the Student Representative Council was in the same English class with me, and she informed me I would only be a couple credits short so I would be allowed to attend graduation. I said as clearly as possible "I will not be participating in the ceremonies." My Grade 12 English teacher informed the entire class that she was very proud of me for attending Grade 12 with students so much younger than me and as a single parent. She, along with my Grade 1 and 2 teachers were my absolute favourite teachers ever. I wish I could remember her name too.

I did go out camping with my new friends from High School after graduation, and the night of the Prom I went to the bar with someone else my age. I saw a student there and I asked him what he was doing there. He said the same thing I was doing, so I figured maybe he was a High School drop-out too who decided to go back after turning 19. A person only had to be 19 years old to go to the bar and drink, and I always found it a fun place to go! My mother would only charge me for babysitting when I wasn't at work or school and before graduation, I started getting these red spots all over my skin. I had no idea what they were, so I went to see the doctor. He told me they were very contagious, and I should take some time off work and not spread it around everywhere. I asked him about camping, and he said that should be alright, so when I saw the owner of Shopper's Drug Mart's son at the campground I didn't think anything of it. When he got back to Yorkton he told his father he saw me camping when I had called in sick to work, so the first day I went back, he fired me. I still had a couple of Grade 12 classes to pass, so I enrolled in those and looked for another job, which didn't take very long at all.

Kyle was enjoying staying at Grandma's house and even found a 'girlfriend' there. Sarah was the daughter of another single parent from Canora, who worked and hired my mother to babysit. Kyle would tell this story that when he was seven years old he was going to marry Sarah and they were going to move into Grandma's house and paint the fridge purple. During the year he was two he was in the hospital every two months for at least a week after he would have another grand mall seizure. Every time I took a night off work, I would lose the pay for that day, so I would go to work and sleep at the hospital in a chair beside my son's crib.

That last semester I enrolled in four classes and I worked at a restaurant called the Lobster Trap. Quite a fancy place and I made pretty good tips but worked for a Greek family who had a daughter a few years younger than me. There was a waitress who worked during the day who trained me to serve tables and treat the customers well. We didn't have uniforms but had to wear a white top and black pants or skirt. I didn't like Lobster, but every other dish in that restaurant smelled so good I would just ignore them and serve the food that smelled so good I could easily ignore the smell of the lobsters. We were allowed to choose one half price meal off the menu to eat during our breaks, and the one dish I will always remember from there is their French fries covered in Greek salad dressing. It tasted like salt and vinegar on fries, but without as much salt and really oily, but yummy.

I worked at the Lobster Trap part-time during the summer and when school started again in the fall I would get up in the morning and go to school for my final four grade 12 classes and go to work in the evenings. Actually, I only needed two more classes to officially get my academic Grade 12, but I thought I'd take a couple more anyway. A full-time position came up working nights at a bar in downtown Yorkton, so I applied, interviewed, and was hired. The owners were teachers and they knew I was still taking Grade 12 classes and raising a son, so they hired me-full-time! I dropped two of my classes, but only so I could continue working full-time until I completed my Grade 12. I did still have to take those caffeine pills to survive all those long hours.

I was very lucky that my mother was working from home looking after other people's children so they could go out to work. While I was working downtown at the bar there was another girl who had a full-time day job in a bank and worked part-time at the same bar. Corinne was living on her own and looking for a roommate, so after I completed my two classes and didn't hear back from S.I.A.S.T., Palliser Campus in Moose Jaw about the accounting program I applied to, we moved into an apartment together with my son. I would take my son over to mother's house when I was about to go to work, or he might sleep there every so often and I would go to her place as soon as I woke up in the morning. Chris found out I was no longer living with my parents, and he drove to Yorkton one night and wanted to spend time with me, but I had decided that I had hurt him enough and he could do so very much better than getting back together with me, so I said good bye to him for the very last time.

> What I learned from this time in my life was to try to get along with everyone, regardless if they were older or younger than me. I was working with people at the bar who were quite a bit older than me, and I got along well with everyone there. When I was at school I found friends to hang around with too, I even dated one guy a few years younger than me for a bit as well. Chris was only 3 years older, as much as David was older than me, but my parents didn't believe that at all, ever. Their loss again.

Chapter Six

From the Frying Pan into the Fire

I WORKED AT THE BAR downtown until another bar opened down the street and I applied to work there. I started working there and also at the Lobster Trap during lunches. During lunches I worked with their daughter, who was the only one that was allowed to work the till by the front door. One time she told me the table that just left gave her a $5 tip and I told her "That was my table!" and she said, "But they left ME the tip." Her parents agreed with her, so I didn't stay much longer at that job. It didn't hurt my feelings too much when Kyle was in the hospital again and I got this horrible nasty headache that sent me into the hospital the day Kyle was released. Good thing he could stay with my parents. I called the bar to let them know I was in the hospital so they could find someone to cover my shift, but I didn't bother calling the Lobster Trap. I figured if their daughter was going to take my tips, she could cover my shift too.

I slept for two days straight in that hospital bed, and I remember waking up once and my roommate and friend Corinne was in the room. I asked her why she didn't wake me and she said, "You looked like you needed the rest and seemed so peaceful." I said I could rest there all day but could only see her for a very short time. I was really glad she showed up. I took to calling her Cori and she told me her sister used to call her Kim while they were growing up. She became another BFF.

While working at that second bar one night I thought Chris came in with a few friends and I served their table but didn't recognize him. I think I recognized a couple of guys at the table, but the whole group left before I could go back to them and see if Chris was with them or not. There were a couple of guys that came into that bar as well, sat in my section, watched me serve them and others and asked if I had ever bartended. I said I hadn't, but I learn quickly. They believed me and asked if I wanted to work for them in a lounge on Broadway beside the bowling alley. I gave my notice at the bar and started working at the lounge and getting a taste of bartending. I LOVED it! Corinne and I decided to rent a huge house with a couple of guys who also worked at the bank. Kyle and I had the whole entire basement to ourselves as a bedroom.

I dated off and on, always one guy at a time, but mother was sick and tired of seeing me date so many different men. She obviously was not prepared by her parents for marriage because she told me that she felt she was raped on her wedding night. David came to Yorkton to stay for a while with his parents. We started dating again and he talked to me about how it would be so very easy to get a job in Alberta near Banff and I was intrigued. We both applied to this lodge and were both hired. Now I had to talk this over with my parents and see if they would allow 3-year-old Kyle to live with them until I could find a place to live and a babysitter in Alberta after I started working there. After I had told Kyle I was going to work at a Lodge in Alberta, he would tell everyone he talked to that his Mommy was working in a 'logs.' I must have been working there for a month when my mother called me and told me Kyle had another Seizure

57

and she had spoken with his doctor about taking his tonsils out. I didn't think that doctors did that anymore, but Mother was sure that having her tonsils removed was what had stopped Karen from having another seizure when she was little. I took the bus to Yorkton and was in the hospital when the surgery was being done and held him after he got out of surgery. The doctor said it went well, and that they removed his tonsils and adenoids and hopefully there would never again be another seizure…but there was. It didn't happen for years, but the surgery did not stop the seizures.

Before Kyle was released from the hospital, I got on the bus again and took it to Banff. David and I both had decided we were done with the lodge and needed to move to Banff where it would be easier to find a babysitter for Kyle when he moved to Alberta. David had no problem finding employment and when I arrived in Banff I was hired as a bartender in a hotel lounge. David would come into that place so often the boss asked me to tell him not to. I told David what my boss had said, and I don't think David believed him, so he kept coming in until the boss had to let me go. David used to drink quite a bit, so I went with him to his first AA meeting in Banff.

I found a daytime job working in a grocery store as a cashier and David was working nights at a restaurant. We started spending time with people we worked with, and I had a colleague who was in the produce department who was from England (I absolutely loved his accent!). He knew another guy who lived at the YMCA and told him he should meet this girl at work (me) because she is really 'fit!' We started spending time together and would often frequent the Elephant and Castle for chicken wings and beer. I found an apartment to move into and I also found a babysitter for Kyle and took the bus to Yorkton and picked him up.

Kyle and John (the friend from the YMCA) got along great and John showed Kyle why he doesn't always have to find a toilet when he has to pee because he's a boy…something that didn't even cross my mind to teach him. Maybe a month later Mother called and she said I got a letter from the school in Moose Jaw. I told her to open it, so she did, and I was accepted into the accounting program I had applied to so long ago. I said I was going to have to think about this, I wasn't sure I wanted to leave Banff. In fact, I knew I didn't want to leave! I asked mother how I was supposed to get there. She said Dad would drive to Banff to pick us up and drop me off in Moose Jaw. I asked her where I was supposed to live and she said Dad would help me find room and board. I asked her where I was supposed to take Kyle and she said he could live with them until I was done school. Even more than not wanting to leave Banff, I didn't want to waitress or be a cashier for the rest of my life, so I agreed. Then…I had to break the news to John.

My roommate agreed to babysit Kyle so John and I could spend one last evening together before we had to leave and go back to Saskatchewan. We went to the Elephant and Castle then walked to the Y.M.C.A. and I fell asleep there, awaking with a start the next morning. OMG! Dad was probably there already, so I had to run! Dad was already there when I got to the apartment, my roommate had to leave for work, so she had let Dad in to watch Kyle. I threw together everything that was mine and we left in quite the hurry. Tears fell as we drove out of the mountains and back into Saskatchewan.

A new chapter in my life was about to begin and in the first few days of school I became friends with the girl one of the staff introduced me to so she could show me around. She was originally from Saskatoon and she was looking for someone with whom to share an apartment. We found an apartment together, walking distance from the school, but she had a car and would drive us in the mornings. She invited me to come to Saskatoon one weekend, so I went. We went to a party with her boyfriend, and I met up with a good-looking guy who used to go to the bars where I worked in Yorkton. He grew up only a half hour North of Yorkton in Canora, SK, but we never met until after High School.

Mark remembered me from the bars in Yorkton and we started hanging out together. I would see him on the weekends I went to Yorkton to visit

Kyle, then see him again in Saskatoon every other weekend. He had taken classes at S.I.A.S.T., Kelsey Campus in Saskatoon to become an X-ray Lab Technician. He was working west of Saskatoon in a small town called Maidstone, and by Christmas we were dating. He told me he had decided to take the Certified Combined Technician course because it was something his father knew nothing about and he was tired of always having to follow his father's orders. That New Year's Eve he was on call, so he invited me to Maidstone to watch the New Year get rung in at different locations on different channels on the T.V. until we fell asleep.

At the end of the school year, I decided to run for President of the Student Representative Council at the college, even though I had never once even considered doing anything like that in High School. I didn't know what to say in my speeches and probably made a complete fool of myself. I invited Mark to join me for the dance and celebration where the winners would be announced. When they announced my opponent's win I walked right over and said, "The better man won!" before shaking the winner's hand and I had to leave before I started crying. I didn't want anyone to see me cry, and Mark drove me to a park, we went for a walk, and he calmed me down. I didn't know what I was trying to prove by running for office, but maybe it was the fear of public speaking I wanted to overcome. The next semester I decided not to go back to college because I had found a job working at the Credit Union in Yorkton and my son was enrolled in kindergarten.

In the middle of that summer Mark asked me if I wanted to go to Kenosee Lake for the August long weekend. I told him I would have to clear that with my parents first. They said no, but I didn't really want to go. He wanted to go alone anyway, so he caught a ride with someone else and was kind enough to leave me his car. But that was IT! I was ready to break up with him. I emptied everything of mine out of his car and gave him his keys when he arrived back after that weekend and I told him I didn't want to see him anymore. But he begged and pleaded, shed some tears and convinced me it was in my best interest to not break up with him.

Also, that summer a friend of his was getting married in a small-town Northwest of Saskatoon and he asked me to be his plus one. I went with him and had a lot of fun at that wedding because I saw Corrine again! It so happened that Mark went to High School with the Groom, and Corinne was dating the bride's brother! I had a bad feeling about that guy right from the very start, but she was in love with him and she was my friend, so I didn't say anything.

Mark and I had sex that night and I suggested he not use a condom because it was at a time of the month I didn't think I could get pregnant. I was wrong. Here I was, pregnant again and still single. I wanted to apply for a job with The Bay up north and disappear, then on October 13, 1989 Mark asked me to marry him. Well, sort of. He stuffed a scrap piece of paper into a fortune cookie on which he had scribbled 'I love you, will you marry me?' He never went down on one knee, nothing romantic, just took the easy way out and dropped off the fortune cookie at the restaurant before picking me up to take me out for dinner and asked me where I wanted to eat. I asked him what he would have done if I didn't want Chinese. He said he would have found a way to convince me. I told him I didn't want to marry him just because I was pregnant with his child, but he said he was planning to ask me in February anyway. I said, "On Valentine's Day?" He said "Yes," and I said, 'Well, I'm glad you didn't!"

We were married on December 2 of that same year because I didn't want to give birth as a single parent again, and Mark agreed to adopt Kyle. We invited all the new friends I made when I went back and finished my Grade 12, I asked Cori to be my Maid of Honour and Mark only had his cousin stand up for him, my father walked me down the aisle, and my eldest sister gave the toast to the bride. Kyle was the ring bearer and his girlfriend from Canora walked beside him as the flower girl. My brother and sister weren't at my wedding because of the distance they lived from Yorkton and the fact it was in the winter. Even though he was an only child, Mark had a whole lot of family and friends who were invited too, his side took up the bigger half of the church. I felt like I got through that entire day out of my body and was watching everything from up above. It was surreal to me.

The next day was gift opening at my parent's place and I drove from there to the place in which we rented to begin our life together. I hit a patch of ice on the highway and ended up in the ditch. Some kind stranger and his wife stopped at the side of the road to see if I was OK. He said he thought he should be able to drive my vehicle out of the ditch, so I gave him my keys and stayed beside his kind wife. When I got to our rented place and told Mark what happened I was still quite shaken up and all he could do was laugh at me. What a way to begin a new marriage. It was actually the third or fourth sign I shouldn't have married him in the first place.

> This was another way of learning things the 'hard' way, but when he was nice to me, he was very nice, and he was so good looking. I thought that I was through with my search for love! Turns out though, I couldn't have been more wrong.

Chapter Seven

M.S.? What's that?

There were many times during the ten and a half years we were married when more signs came up, but he was my husband and I didn't want to fail my children by leaving their father. Mark never did adopt Kyle or treat him like his own son, even when we moved to a small town outside of Regina where someone he worked with said they could see a lot of Mark in Kyle. Besides my father, Mark was basically the only other father figure in Kyle's life to this point, so he learned how to be angry and spoiled. Mark's mother didn't want him to call her grandma until after our daughter was born in April of 1990 and learning to call her Jean, because that's what her big brother called her. Then she said she wanted them to both call her Grandma Jean.

We moved at least three times that first year, first to Wolseley where Mark found work, then to an apartment in Yorkton when he was hired at a private lab. I had trouble finding work, so I enrolled in an Income Tax Preparation course through H & R Block. His father bought a house for us to move into and it was really close for the kids to walk to school, and only a block away from my parent's place. I found a full-time job working shifts at the hospital in Dietary. I had already moved up to the Bakeshop when both of my parents decided to retire. I'm sure she would have, but I didn't want to ask my mother to watch her grandkids after she retired, so I found a woman who worked with me in Dietary and asked her if she would bring her son to my place if I decided to stay home and babysit. She said, "sure I would!" so I decided to quit my bakeshop job at the hospital and stay home with my young children while watching other people's kids to continue to contribute financially to our home.

During that time I was with my children 24/7, so I needed to get out once in a while on weekends. Mark took me out one weekend and we joined up with friends of mine at a bar. When the bar closed, we all decided to go to a friend of mine's place for a party. This just happened to be on a weekend when a friend of Mark's drove in from out of town to visit. We got a sitter and the three of us piled into the back seat of a car, and someone from the front seat asked if one of us from the back would please move to the front seat because there was room on his knee. Not thinking I was hurting anyone or doing anything wrong, I offered to, got out of the back seat and climbed into the front and sat on someone else's knee, thinking I was helping to fit more people into the car to get to the party. When we got there and everyone got out of the car I was looking in the back seat for my purse, and someone said they saw it in the snowbank beside the car. I went into the house to ask Mark why he threw it into the snow and he opened his mouth and he actually bit me on my nose! We all had had quite a lot to drink so I was going through the house yelling at everyone he bit my nose. Someone called a cab for me and told me to go home and lock the doors. I did that, and went to bed, but a couple of hours later when I heard knocking at the door, I opened it up and let him and his friend in.

After doing childcare for a few years just before it was time to enroll our daughter in Kindergarten, Mark decided we should expand our family!

I thought I might like to have another child, even though I knew how much childbirth hurt. I thought maybe we should just get a dog, but I also wondered what it might be like to want to add a child to the family even before they were conceived. We continued having unprotected sex quite often. It didn't take long at all to get the good news from our family doctor that we were expecting again! Kyle was five and a half years older than Chelsea, and Angeline was born in October of 1994, four and a half years after Chelsea. From April 29 until October 13 all my kids are exactly five years apart.

Mark fell asleep during the last hour of labour for his first daughter even after being told that was the most important time to be beside your wife and support her. When his second daughter was born he came into the hospital when I was about ready to deliver and gave my friend Nancy heck for being there with me. He refused to even ask the nurses to check how far I was dilated, so I had to walk to the nurses' desk and ask them before they rushed me into the delivery room. My third baby's arm got stuck in the birth canal and the doctor looked stressed as I was trying to push her out. After our baby was born it looked to me like Mark's eyebrows were on the ceiling and his jaw on the floor. I jumped up and screamed "What's WRONG?" He moaned quietly "It's a girl!" Our doctor told us he was sure I was carrying just like I would carry a boy, so that must have been what Mark's heart was set on. Oh well, I was happy with another girl, and I was pretty sure he'd get used to it.

He did nice things for me too, like buying two tickets to see the Phantom of the Opera with him in Regina after he heard me say that's what I wanted. He purchased a card and put the tickets inside it and under my pillow to surprise me. We took a trip to Disney World when Chelsea was only 18 months old. She stayed in Canora with Grandma Jean who toilet trained her before we got back. We took my nephew Cameron with us to babysit so we could have some 'alone time' which we never had because we were all always so busy being tourists.

He also travelled with me to Nanaimo so I could be in Karen's wedding. I was her Matron of Honour because I was already married, but there was just her sister and me in the wedding party. I didn't mention to Mark that I had dated both her brothers, but I did see them at the wedding. Her father started yelling at us when we started packing up to transport things back to their home, because he said people are going to think this party is over. I grabbed his arm and said "Let's dance, then people will know it's not over, OK?" Steve later said he couldn't believe how tough I was to get his father to stop yelling, and I told him he should be happy he had a father like Joe. I had learned their Mom had been married to their birth father who was an alcoholic, then left him taking their four kids and married Joe, who became the father those kids never had...a wonderful man.

I will never forget the earrings I picked out in Nanaimo while we were there. Every store we went into I would look at these sparkly earrings made with crystal, but I couldn't find any I liked enough to purchase for myself until I found 1 pair of heart-shaped studs for $9.99. Mark yelled at me not to buy them because he had already bought me a pair. I put the earrings back and still regret putting them back to this day. The ones he bought me were dangly, and I usually like dangly earrings, but those earrings sparkled so much they didn't need to be dangly. The ones I left behind were just little hearts that sat right on an earlobe.

I had purchased cloth diapers to let my babies wear until they were toilet-trained, and they were quite expensive. I remember waking up one morning and not being able to find them. I asked where they were and Mark informed me he had thrown them in the garbage. I asked him why and he said they were costing him too much in water and electricity for the use of the washer and dryer. No discussion with me at all, I just had to accept what he wanted the entire time we were married. Just like when he took me to test-drive vans then decided himself, without discussing it with me, that we would trade the little car I had been driving in for a van that I didn't like.

After Angeline turned about eight months old Mark drove us to a Dinosaur Park to meet my sister halfway between Yorkton, where we were living, and Edmonton, where they lived. I brought all three kids and she brought her two youngest. She had met a doctor in Victoria, dated him for a while then married him. Cameron and Traci gained another set of siblings, a sister Natasha and a younger brother Jacob. They lived in a fabulous designer house in Edmonton, right across the street from the University hospital. But when we arrived at the park, Mark set up our tent then left us there because he needed to go back home to work.

Also, after Angeline was born I got a call from a neighbour, one of Kyle's French teachers who lived across the back alley from us and just had a baby girl around the same age as Angeline. She was wondering if I knew anyone who would babysit. I said I didn't and hung up the phone. After thinking about it, I called her back and asked her if she would trust me with her daughter and she said that was actually why she called me. One more child in the house, the same age as my baby was not something I felt would be too difficult for me to handle.

I did that for one school year while Mark was making arrangements to move our family to Canora. I said I didn't think he wanted to take over his family's farm because of why he told me he took the course at Kelsey. But he enticed me to look at new houses he would have built on his father's land for his family. I started getting excited to move, then one morning in June I woke up nauseous. We made arrangements for my mother to watch the girls and Mark took me to the hospital.

The doctor sent me to emergency at the Plains hospital in Regina to see a Neurologist. The Neurologist did a Lumbar Puncture and told me I needed to lay flat for 24 hours afterwards, so they admitted me. Mark stayed at his Aunt and Uncle's place for the night and after he left the hospital, a Neurologist came into my room and told me he suspected M.S. He said he couldn't diagnose me because the first word in M.S. is multiple and they only saw one attack so far.

The next morning my Neurologist came into the room and told us both to go home and put it out of our minds as I may never have another attack. But she did tell us to please give her a call if anything different happens. That day on the way home my left hand went numb. The pins and needles felt like I had cut off the circulation, so I kept shaking my hand to get the blood flowing again. When I was still feeling the pins and needles a week later I thought, well, this is something different, maybe I should call her again, so I did. She asked us to please come back to the Plains hospital in Regina. She was going to admit me that day, so we stayed longer than we needed to, but she told us we had an appointment at the Royal University Hospital in

Saskatoon for an M.R.I. in two months. She said she was going to admit me so I might be able to get in sooner, but they had no appointments any sooner. So we went to Saskatoon two months later and had the M.R.I. done. It was Multiple Sclerosis, my doctor confirmed over the phone. He probably did try to explain it to me a bit, but I heard nothing after the words Multiple Sclerosis.

While living in Canora in his parent's home, Mark would always complain about how his father was only giving him the bare minimum amount of money to survive and we were living in poverty. The one time I mentioned that to his parents in front of him, he said out loud to them "But they are paying our power, energy and phone bills, so everything is just fine." I was only saying what he had been complaining to me about constantly, but when I brought it up to his parents, he took their side.

That Christmas Mark purchased a couple of tickets for us to fly out east to visit Rachel and her husband and new baby in Hamilton. He also made arrangements for us to stay a night or two at my Aunt and Uncle's place in Oshawa. I was happy to see my friends and family, but was worried about flying with MS. I didn't know a whole lot about the disease that was about to become my new normal. He mentioned that he had bought tickets for the two of us to see a professional hockey game, but he didn't tell me how high up our seats were. He said he had also purchased insurance on the flights in case I was too sick and I said I was, but he said that I wasn't in the hospital, so we should go. I really didn't want to go, but went anyway.

That same year after a big fight before he went to work at a hospital in a neighbouring town, Mark got quite upset with me and threw me against a plant stand, spilling dirt everywhere. After he left I cleaned everything up, packed a few bags and decided to go to a shelter in Yorkton with my children. That was the beginning of the end. We separated quite a few times after that but kept getting back together so often that I thought nothing could ever tear us apart.

During times when our marriage really felt like it was falling apart, I started noticing how badly Mark would treat Kyle. Our children were probably very confused and upset about the problems in our marriage, but Mark made sure he never pushed or hit me in front of them. I tried to cry as little as I could in front of them too, because of what my nurse sister told me when Kyle was a baby and sick in the hospital. Kyle was probably feeling left out with all the attention we needed to give his sisters that he would do all kinds of things that 14+ year old boys do, but Mark was never very forgiving of Kyle.

When staying at the shelter with my children, I would see all three of them cuddled up on the swing in the back yard, getting along so much better than they ever did in Canora. One of the workers at the shelter said it's probably because the girls would see their father yelling at and beating on Kyle that they didn't dare get cuddly with him in front of their father, for fear of the same thing happening to them. I had to go to a support group meeting and Kyle had already been through the babysitting course, so the workers at the shelter said it would be OK with them if Kyle stayed at the shelter and babysat. When I got back to the shelter after the meeting the worker told me how impressed she was with how quickly Kyle responded to Angeline's tears. I figured he was going to be a great father one day, even after the negative influence of Mark.

Mark bought a house in Yorkton for us to move into, without even considering looking at a house I was interested in because he said he thought that people would think we lost money when we moved to the farm. But we did! I never knew why he didn't want people to know that, but I didn't want to argue, I just wanted our family back together. Kyle was so upset living in that house that he would steal my van, act up in school and treat us in all kinds of negative ways that neither of us wanted our daughters to learn, so we found a boarding school in Regina to send Kyle to. Luther College was connected to the University of Regina too, so going to Luther would give him leg up to get into the university after he completed grade twelve.

Mark mentioned once that if I ever left him again it would be the last time. I didn't believe him, he had already told me so very many lies. After I told him I found an apartment, he stole my house key off my keychain, took our girls to his parent's place in Canora and threw me out of the house that he used to tell me he wanted me to think of as mine. It never did feel like home. The first day I spent 24 hours alone after being married for ten and a half years was the date I used as my password for everything for a long time after that (06/28/00). I slept on the couch I had to buy to put in the living room along with the dining table and chairs. I had to pay for all the furniture, blankets, pillows, dishes, pots and pans and basically everything I needed to set up a home. Mark asked for a list of things I needed from the home and I gave him one, not realizing he meant that was going to be my share of half the belongings from the house. I felt like he had thrown me out with less than I entered that marriage, but my children were at least with me half of the time... for a while.

Not even four months later Mark started sleeping with a girl I used to work with at the hospital. She had married a friend of mine and I thought she was my friend too, until she started rubbing it in my face that she was sleeping with my husband. She had cheated on my friend with his best friend and broke up her own marriage and now here she was getting in between my husband and me. She even bought a winter coat that was exactly the same one my older daughter had purchased for herself. She won my daughters over shortly after starting to sleep with my husband because...well, I don't know what was going through her head. It just felt like another stab in the back every time I saw or even thought of the two of them together. He probably told her, because I often heard him say that I GOT PREGNANT so he would marry me...like it only takes one person to get pregnant. I didn't bother to bring up the fact that when he asked me to marry him I told him I didn't want to get married just because I was pregnant and he said he was going to ask me the following February anyway. He basically had to convince me to take that step.

I applied at many places and didn't have any luck finding a job this time, so I decided to apply to university into the field of Social Work. I looked forward to replacing those who did me so very wrong all those years ago, and maybe joining those who spoke to me like a human being for the first time ever. I was lucky that I had kept taking university classes, one per year as my children grew up, and the classes from S.I.A.S.T. counted towards a few first-year university classes too. I was accepted into Social Work, and I kept applying for jobs until I found one I could do part-time while taking full-time classes and raising my children half the time while struggling with M.S. and the divorce. Mark was doing everything he could think of to stab me in the back because he wanted custody of the girls so he wouldn't have to pay child support. I took to volunteering too, hoping to get some experience in Social Work type positions.

Kyle was asked to leave Luther College and he moved into the apartment with me. I had rented a three-bedroom apartment at the time, so I had to buy bunkbeds for the girls to sleep in the master bedroom, and a double for Kyle to sleep on in the second bedroom. He was still a teenager, and still angry, so he brought some friends home from school one day when I wasn't working and the whole group of them brought in a dozen beer with them. Even though Kyle was younger than me, he was getting taller than me and with a group of his friends, so I decided to sit down and drink a beer with them so they wouldn't even consider beating me up. I thought better they drink here and not out in public, but looking back, I should have known better. That was one of the many stupid things I did when I was alone again. Then one day he was angry with me and was chasing me around the apartment (while the girls were at their father's place), so I went into the bathroom and locked the door. He was so angry he broke it down and scared me so much that I went that day to the police and pressed charges.

I went with the R.C.M.P. to the apartment to let them in and I walked away. They handcuffed Kyle and took him into custody, then called Child

Protection, who called my parents and placed Kyle with them. When he had a court date, I went to the courthouse so I could be there for him. He talked to his Legal Aid lawyer then left the courthouse. I went to the lawyer to let him know that Kyle had left and asked him if he told Kyle to leave and the lawyer said he didn't. He asked me if I wanted to appear on his behalf and I said no, I didn't think that would teach him anything. When the judge got to Kyle's name the Lawyer said his mother is here but doesn't want to appear on his behalf.

The judge called my name and asked me to stand, so I did. He then asked if I was Kyle's mother and I said yes, then he inquired, "But you don't want to answer for him?"

I said, "No your honour, I do not."

He then said OK, you can sit down, and he issued a warrant for Kyle's arrest. A counsellor who worked with alcoholics saw the whole thing and met me at the door as I was leaving the courtroom. He asked me if I was OK and if I had support at home with me. Even though I didn't, I said "Yes, I'll be fine. Thank you." He told me that was a very courageous thing to do, but it was the right thing. I answered, "I know that, but thanks again." The counsellor seemed to want me to stay and talk with him, but I felt I needed to get out of there, so I just went home and cried all alone...again.

I dated off and on and usually only when my children were with their father until I felt close enough to a guy that I thought our relationship might last. I jumped into dating the first guy far too quickly and was forced to break up with him pretty quickly too. I didn't like the way he always grabbed my ass anyway — very, very disrespectful — but I didn't respect myself either at that point. When you go a lifetime of nobody showing you respect of any kind what-so-ever, it takes a very long, long time to learn to respect yourself. Volunteering also helped me learn to respect myself.

I took every Social Work class that I had heard of since being a child in foster care, which is possibly why I passed everything I did pass. There was one teacher who taught me first year Sociology by standing at the front of the class and lecturing. Nothing he said made much sense to me, it mostly consisted of dates, just like the social studies class in Grade 10 that I failed, dropped out of and finally passed when a super teacher taught it to me... finally! I failed a few university classes, so I either took them again and passed, or took a different class if the one I didn't pass wasn't a requirement. Life goes on, right?

I volunteered with Big Brothers and Big Sisters in Yorkton and accepted a position on their Board. I also did the books for a church Chelsea wanted us to attend. It was Evangelical I think and I had always felt I would allow my children to decide which religion they wanted to follow when they were old enough to decide for themselves.

> I had difficulty raising all my children on my own, but it was even sadder when I had to live alone while they were with their father and his girlfriend then wife. I learned M.S. was not just a physical condition, but a psychologically draining one as well. I kept taking anti-depressants because I knew I wouldn't be able to get over it on my own, but I also made many mistakes raising my children when they were with me. I would put their dad down and say mean things about his 'lover.' I completely understand why they don't want to spend time with me any more.

Chapter Eight

Diamond When I Die

I WOULD HAVE CONVOCATED IN June of 2003, but my M.S. flared up during my first attempt at a major Practicum in a government office. I did one mini practicum in a school with a Social Worker who was tough on me, but I did get through it as well as the other classes I took that semester. I started my Major the next semester but it was so hot that my M.S. started to react to the heat. I remember feeling like I was melting and especially driving home... or anywhere for that matter. The Supervisor in the office didn't like me from the very first day and I could feel her hatred directed at me everywhere in that office. I had to take a medical leave from studies and was only allowed to take three classes the following semester. I also wasn't allowed to try another practicum, so I just took a couple of electives in different colleges like Education, Kinesiology and Women's Studies. If I couldn't get through my second try at a major Practicum, I would have at least experienced different colleges and I'd be able to decide which one I wanted to pursue.

I did sit across the desk from a really nice man who I was sad to leave when I was told my practicum was over. In chatting with him over breaks and things I found out he lived right across the street from my parent's house. Bob and his wife Connie had two sons and were worried when their boys were outside playing street hockey that the older couple across the street were going to complain their boys were too loud. One day as he watched my mother walk across the street towards him, he prepared himself to stand up for his kids, but the old lady (my mother) had come across the street to let the neighbours know that they were really happy to hear their boys playing outside instead of being glued to a computer or gaming system.

As it turned out, I chose a Safe Shelter for battered women and their children to do my second try at a major practicum. I didn't choose the shelter I stayed at every time I left the marital home with my children. I walked into the First Nations shelter in Yorkton and spoke with the Social Worker working there. I had such a super great learning experience for those four months. I saw there were a lot of First Nations people needing Social Workers, and some who became Social Workers because that's who helped them shape their lives. I learned a whole new culture and admired the elders and all those I met with a career, a family or both. Plus I knew how they felt when they had to leave their home. I put together a program for the young children combining my knowledge of the kids I used to look after and the Social Work I had learned.

After graduating with my bachelor's, I found a term position in a place called Partners in Employment for a few months and the first day without a job I walked back into the shelter I had finished my degree through and asked them if they were hiring. They said yes, but this is all we can offer and she wrote a figure down. It was quite low, but I thought, well, I was never one to "Go for the Money!" so I said I could work with that. I was starting to make payments on my student loans that weren't forgiven as some were because I was a single parent. The next semester I decided to take a women's studies class in the evening, but I didn't need a loan for it. While working at that shelter I read an ad in the newspaper that someone (in fact, one of the girls who was with the group of kids that showed up with Kyle and beer that afternoon at my place) had just given birth to my first grandchild! I got a message to her telling her I would love to meet them, and maybe even babysit at some point. Kyle was in jail when his son was born, and she knew how angry Kyle was with me, so she waited until he was out and told him I was interested in babysitting for them so together, they brought him over to where I was living.

Before Christmas an ad came out for students with a bachelor's degree to apply to a graduate level course the college was bringing to the Yorkton Campus. I went in to talk to an advisor about trying for another bachelor's compared to applying to get into the master's level program. She said another degree would only help me if I got a job in the education system. A master's would help more no matter where I found employment, so I applied. The masters was in Adult Education and you had to have a degree and some experience teaching. Well, my argument was that counselling at the shelter was just like teaching and the university agreed and accepted me into the program!

I was so very excited when I opened the acceptance letter that I remember Angeline getting scared and running to the kitchen where I was to ask me why I was screaming, what was wrong, and if I was OK. I gushed 'Oh baby, I'm more than just OK, I just got accepted into the master's level program!" It was right around that time that the Tribal Council I was working for decided to send all of their employees to a work retreat at a Lodge near a lake that was only an hour away. We would be gone for three days and that's when Chelsea decided to move in with her father and his second wife, and she may have stayed with me overnight only once or twice after that. We had just moved into an apartment in a huge house that had been divided up into three or four different suites and I don't think she liked it right from the start. I think that Chelsea was disappointed in me because I had just finished studying and I already had a degree. She had no idea why I wanted to continue studying instead of spending time with my children. My children were with their father and his second wife half the time and I felt I needed to keep busy.

I would be so hurt every time I'd see or think of the two of them together that I probably did say many hurtful things about them in front of my children, so eventually they all disowned me. Who would really want to live with a bitter single parent over a couple newlyweds anyway? I asked Angeline if she would ever consider moving to Regina with me. I said she would still be able to graduate with the kids she started school with in Kindergarten, but asked her how she felt about moving to Regina every second year for Grades 9 and 11. She said "Sure!" and sounded really excited about it. I moved into an apartment close to the High School she chose and even enrolled her while she was still in Grade 8.

So the Catholic High School in Yorkton was where she was also enrolled that same year. Her father enrolled her in Yorkton and wouldn't go back to court to get this figured out until after the school year for her Grade 9 started. I couldn't afford to fight him and his wife who both worked and contributed to their household, and he could afford to take me to court to squeeze every penny from me that they possibly could. They wouldn't include me in the plans for the classes Chelsea would take in university, where she would live, how she would get to Winnipeg, or any information at all about her first year of university. But, I guess they figured she had a step-mom, why bother including the person who carried her under her heart for nine months, breast fed her for 18 months and woke up with her every night when her father wouldn't because he had to wake up and go off to work in the mornings.

When I did take him back to court to see if I could get the Child Support I had to pay lowered, he and his lawyer figured out a way to make me pay even more than I already was. It didn't matter that I had car payments, student loans, and rent to pay every month. They both contributed to their grocery bills, his father paid for their house and they probably didn't have car loans any more either. I was seeing a counsellor who seemed to me to be happy when

I would cry. I asked her why she was smiling as I am wiping my tears away and she said "Tears are healing. You are going through so much pressure in your life right now, by the time you depart from this world, you'll be a diamond."

I made many friends in Yorkton even after I was separated. Mark and Suzie did try to turn as many people against me as they could, but I met people through school, my part-time jobs, volunteer work, my practicums, the Church we started attending with Chelsea, and so on. I always seemed to run into one of them though, and it was like another stab in my heart every single time. Whether I would see her at the florist's while buying flowers for Angeline's 11th birthday or I would see her driving my husband's truck, I needed to get out of that city. Especially after signing the divorce papers and hearing that my ex remarried so quickly. I couldn't sign those papers at home through the tears that were flowing because I thought about how we had promised to love, honour and respect each other until death do we part. We had children, but he had Suzie now. So sad.

I reconnected with Cori and her husband who had a baby daughter that died one morning just eating breakfast. I took the girls to her funeral and both my daughters cried huge tears for that poor little sweetie. Cori and her husband had separated, but after the funeral they did get back together to grieve and try for more children. They gave birth to twin girls in 2007 which was the same year I only had one more class in my Graduate course before I could complete it.

> From this chapter in my life I learned that keeping busy during my separation was keeping me sane, and I'm actually glad I was diagnosed. I'm also glad I had a son so young and that my father convinced me to go back to High School to get an academic Grade twelve. And I learned there are worse things than divorce, like watching your 18 month old child die right in front of you, like Cori had to. I was having exacerbations while I was married and stressed out, but going through my divorce I had some problems with heat, but no stress from living with my husband so no actual M.S. flares.

Chapter Nine

Moving on UP!

I PHONED CORINNE AND ASKED her if she wanted some help with her babies for a bit. She asked if I might be able to stay for a month. I asked her if I could stay for longer while I look for work and a place to live in Regina. That's what I did when I moved to Regina in the beginning of September when Angeline started her last year of Junior

High in Grade 8 and Chelsea was in Grade 12. As soon as Cori's husband talked to me alone, he asked me how long I was planning to stay, because many women have twins and raise them alone. By October 1, 2007 I had two full-time jobs and a place to live in Regina.

One job was looking after a severely challenged adult female who needed assistance 24 hours a day. They needed me to sleep at her house and they would also pay me hourly for looking after her in the evenings when her other roommate had the night off. She had a full-time worker during the days and during those days I found a job at Regina Alternative Measures Program. Once at R.A.M.P. it was decided to have a feast and round dance one evening that I was supposed to be working with Ashleigh. I talked to both bosses and everyone agreed I should take Ashleigh to the dance and she had a blast!

At R.A.M.P. I went to provincial court every morning for a week and everyone referred to R.A.M.P. that week became my client. Each worker in that office went to court for a full week every month and the court would refer people who committed their first crime, and/or something maybe not so serious. We would do mediations and come to an agreement between the accused and the victims. Each would have a chance to share their thoughts and feelings around the incident in which the accused was charged for being involved.

By April of 2008 I found an apartment near the High School, Angeline and I had stopped at for her to enroll in for Grade 9. I started Volunteer work a year later after being hired at R.A.M.P. to start up and run the Serious Offence Program in 2009. That program had a group of professionals in the community who would come together once every quarter and form the Advisory Committee. I would run this meeting every three months or so and the members included the Chief of Police in the city, the Head of Prosecution for the Provincial Court, The Victim Services Coordinator, the Executive Director of R.A.M.P., sometimes even Board Members of R.A.M.P., etc.

I also volunteered through a church with newly released adult criminals who had done time in prison for very serious crimes. They didn't want to go back to the lifestyle that led them to commit the crimes in the first place and get sent back to jail. I would get together with Professors from the university who would have coffee and snacks with the one of the guys and talk to him like the human being he was. We helped him find a job, a place to live, and be able to speak without having to use swear words. We were trying to get him back out on the street, but with different thoughts, values and ideas than he had been holding all his life. I even said once that I loved the walking path around the lake, but I would never go there alone and he asked me "Why not?" I said "I'm female, single, relatively small and not all that physically strong."

He offered to go with me and said he would protect me, so I took him up on that offer. He walked all the way around the lake with me, his head held high and so very proud to be protecting someone else! I think we both felt good that day.

I found another casual job supervising parents visits with their children that needed to be supervised because of a court order. I would have to take notes on what everyone said, but not word for word, just if the words were inappropriate. I was juggling three jobs, a bunch of volunteer work, visiting with my daughter every second weekend and paying for every one of her trips to and from Regina, groceries, rent, my car loan, my student loan, the list goes on. Someone I admire told me I should just quit all my jobs and tell the courts I can't afford to pay child support which supports my ex and his second wife. I told the person I've been a single parent before and know how expensive kids are. Plus, if I quit all my jobs, how would my loans get paid? How would I eat or pay rent?

I was at work when I checked my Facebook at lunch and I had received a message from Rachel's husband saying thanks for the Christmas card, but Rachel passed away last October. He had told me she was sick and I was so busy with my failed marriage and scramble for education and work that I hadn't made the time to call her. I was absolutely devastated and became even more depressed. I had hated the fact that Mark had made me travel after my devastating diagnosis, but I had to thank him (in my heart, not in person) for taking me to see her one last time. Her son was 14 when she died.

I would have graduated in June of that year, but I had failed another class by two points. I needed a 70% to pass every master's level class and my Professor felt I had only earned 68%. He actually did try to raise my grade by two, but the university wouldn't let him. He wasn't teaching that class in the next semester but felt bad so he taught only me that class and asked me to summarize a certain textbook about the material from the class. I had to pay for it again, and the Prof knew I knew the information from the class, but he needed me to put my knowledge on paper to show his bosses that I did know the material. I think it was failing that class that made me realize every time I did something wrong or not well enough, I would consider it a lesson I knew I needed to learn.

I put my profile on a dating site and looked around for someone to date while I was finishing all my graduate-level courses so I could graduate in October of 2008. I dated a guy who lived near enough to walk over to his place, it was only a few short blocks away. We spent time walking around Wascana Lake in the city, at his fire pit outside in his back yard and watching movies of all kinds and some TV shows, like Dexter. We did attend the less expensive theatre near where we lived once or twice, but we mostly watched the TV at his place.

I met his daughter as did Angeline when she came to Regina with a friend of hers to see me convocate with my masters in June of 2008. He had a friend of his burn the convocation ceremony onto a DVD for me and I thanked him profusely.

My new family doctor in Regina kept hearing from me that I had been diagnosed with MS and she asked me if I was seeing a Neurologist, and I said I wasn't. She referred me to see one in Regina because if I do have MS I should have at least one Neurologist who knows my past history, so I went. That Neurologist asked me why I was diagnosed with MS and I told him from the MRI because I had forgotten all about the lumbar puncture they had done 12 years earlier. He said that MRIs can show the same things that appear for many different reasons and he wanted to talk to my doctor to find out why I was diagnosed with MS and see me again in six months.

In six months' time I asked the guy I was seeing to come with me to see the doctor, so he did. We were waiting in one of the examination rooms and the Neurologist walked in and said "So, what did you find out?" I got upset with him and told him he said he was going to talk to my doctor and ask him why I was diagnosed! The Neurologist told me he still thinks I was misdiagnosed, and I should just go home and not worry about it. I started crying and he said "this is good news, why are you crying?" The guy I was with told him I always cry and the doctor said not to worry about it. Then for some reason, I'm not even sure why —even to this day — we stopped spending time together. I asked a colleague at work to help me transfer his couches he had lent me back to his place, and it was over.

I went back to my family doctor's office and asked her for some Celexa to combat the depression I was feeling. I kept going back to her office every three to six months or so and telling her that the dose wasn't high enough, I was still crying almost every day. In fact, I cried in her office as I was telling her what my moods were like. The last time I went into her office and asked her for a higher dose, she told me that she would put me on the highest dose I could get, and if that didn't work we would have to try a different drug. I had already tried so many anti-depressants in the past and had such negative reactions that I didn't want to go back on any of them.

Rent in the apartment I was living was about to go up and I saw a basement suite being offered for the same amount of rent I was paying, so I went over to look at it. It was a lawyer who was my age but working in a law firm in the city. I moved into her basement, cut her grass once or twice and stayed alone in her house when she had to travel for work or went on a holiday. She remembered seeing me in court and I explained to her where I worked. After staying there for a few months I started feeling uncomfortable with having no windows through which I could leave in case of a fire, and Sheila, my boss at work, knew of a place where I could rent a room for less money per month.

After spending a couple years alone I started seeing another guy who lived about four hours away, we would communicate through the computer and over the phone, because that's how he preferred it. He was delightfully funny and I thought he was tall and entertaining. We spent a week at my timeshare in BC for our second date and then dated for about three years after that. He had been married twice and had at least a couple children from both marriages. One of his adult daughters lived in Regina and he would visit with her when he drove into the city. We went to watch an acting festival in the Cathedral area in Regina and I met his dog and his daughter with her son.

He had adult daughters from his first marriage, and he had three younger children from his second marriage. Both of his wives had moved out of the house he had purchased for his family and right in with another guy. He did get to see his younger kids and spend time with them, so I met them too. I remember him driving all of us somewhere and Munchie (his dog) came and sat on my lap like he owned me. It was the first time in a long time that I felt like I was part of a 'family' again, but this time one in which I was actually happy!

From this chapter I learned dating doesn't last forever, but can actually be fun! I was like a friend I knew in Junior High School, dating different men, but taking my time and being picky, not just falling for the 'best looking' guy any more.

Chapter Ten

Two Steps Forward, One Step Back

I APPLIED FOR A GOVERNMENT position near where he lived and I got an interview. I was hired for a term position in the city and found a house in which a lady was renting out a room. I left a bunch of boxes of my belongings at his place because I had moved out of my own apartment in Regina into a house where I was only renting one room. A friend in Regina offered his basement for me to store a bunch of things in too, so at one time I felt everything I owned was spread all over the place.

I didn't have any movers because I couldn't afford it, so with only what could fit in one room, and my belongings needing to be stored elsewhere, I was at my boyfriend's house putting my belongings in his basement and drove the four hours back and forth two or three times that weekend before I started work on Monday morning. I was incredibly tired, but as far as I knew, I didn't have Multiple Sclerosis anymore, so I knew I needed to just handle it. The guy whose position I was taking over was trying to train me and my eyes kept closing, he thought I was sleeping! He told our boss that and she kept a close watch on me for that entire term. She didn't like me right from the start either.

Angeline drove to Dafoe one weekend so she could spend one night in North Battleford with me. Dafoe was not halfway, but she had just gotten her driver's license and I was driving everywhere I had to be since June 28, 2000, the first day after I was locked out of 'our' house. We spent our final night together for the next chapter of our lives one summer day in 2012, after she graduated and before she started her post-secondary schooling at Algonquin in Ontario.

I was running out of my Antidepressants and there were no doctors taking new patients. I went to the Medi-Clinic where doctors in the city took turns working three or four hour shifts for all those who could not get a family doctor. The doctor who saw me said he could give me a refill, but when I am taking this kind of drug, I should be seeing a Psychiatrist. No doctors in North Battleford, but Psychiatrists all over the place because of the huge Sanitarium built just outside the city. I saw that doctor, told her my story, and she referred me to a Neurologist in Saskatoon. I went to see her and told her my story after which she ordered another two MRIs. Then my boyfriend dropped me off at the Royal University Hospital in Saskatoon so I could have another MRI or two done. The results confirmed my original diagnosis.

Before I even knew the results of those tests, I decided to invite him to my niece's wedding in Kelowna. He came with me and met my sister, nephews and nieces that were her kids, and is in pictures from that day that will be saved for a lifetime. My nephew asked me to dance and the whole time he was talking to me about how he will never forget me giving him this little furry toy dog I had that barked and then flipped over when Cameron was five. He brought tears to my eyes - happy tears – but they didn't look like I was happy when the dance was over. He gave me a huge, long hug before he let me go sit back down. Cameron is the same nephew whose first belly laugh in his life was when I did a cartwheel in his parent's living room.

Connie's other son at that same dance asked me to dance a couple times and said he was thrilled that he was dancing with someone who knew all the words to each song that was played! It was mostly classic rock and music I listened to when I was his age and if I knew the words, I was singing! Nobody could hear me anyway thank goodness, because not everyone likes the sound of my voice as much as I do. I thought we had fun at that wedding until I fell in the parking lot on the way to where the car was parked. No major flares, but degeneration bit by bit.

We also had to stop at a field of cherry trees because there was a big sign that invited people in to pick their own cherries. After picking a little bit, the mosquitoes and heat were getting to me so I said I was ready to go now. He said "No! This is my vacation too." I realized when he said that we had been spending most of this holiday with my family and he wants to do some stuff too, so I shouldn't try to stop him. We stayed until he was ready to go and we both had lots of freshly picked cherries to take home.

That term position didn't last, but a friend of mine who I went to university classes with in Yorkton called me and told me he could see that my term was almost over and he wanted to know if I wanted a job working with him in Post-Adoptions. I said if I could do it from where I was living and he said "No, you'd have to move back to Regina." The people I worked with in the North Battleford office thanked me before I left for taking the boss's eyes off of them and being the one in the office that she concentrated all of her hatred on. So by the following October, I did move back to Regina. My boyfriend and I had dated before when I was living in Regina, I was sure we could do it again.

We didn't spend a whole lot of time together, but he travelled to Yorkton before Christmas to meet my daughters, my other sister, her husband and my parents. He met my other sister and family at her oldest daughter's wedding in Kelowna and I thought this was THE guy I was ready to spend the rest of my life with. My sisters liked him, my daughters didn't find anything that they complained to me about him, and dad spent a long time in the living room asking him about his family and telling him about being a mechanic and then teaching mechanics until he retired.

I was trying to get my child support payments lowered, but couldn't afford a lawyer so I represented myself. I didn't win anything when I took my ex back to court, probably because I didn't mention anything about my diagnosis of M.S. being confirmed. Sheila was my boss at R.A.M.P. where I worked before moving to North Battleford. She had lots of experience in court and she came with me once... well, she met me in Yorkton. We had a lunch at Mom's and Sheila said it was like a Christmas feast at her place!

There was a woman I met while working with that severely disabled adult female in Regina who was selling her condo but had already moved to Saskatoon. I only paid for the power and energy I used while I was there and I promised her I would clean up after eating breakfast every morning and leave it in the condition it needed to be in for the realtors to show it to prospective buyers.

While living and working in Regina I kept sending my resume to positions that opened up in North Battleford. A position opened as a case-worker assistant in the Child Protection division in NB, so I applied and was accepted there. I did that job for a full year and it was the most depressing division to work in, especially after working in Post-adoptions in Regina. In Post adoptions my clients would call or e-mail me thanking me for just doing my job! In Child Protection the clients would yell, scream and swear at me when I was there assisting to apprehend their children.

We really didn't spend a whole lot of time together the next year, but I stayed at his place for New Year's Eve with his three youngest children and we all went over to his mother's place and met his mother and her friend on New Year's Day. The following year though, we saw even less of each other until he ghosted me and would not return my calls, wouldn't reply to any e-mail or text and just stopped talking to me altogether. My youngest daughter graduated that May and that's when I found out that my boyfriend didn't want to see me anymore.

I was devastated…but it was understandable I suppose. I wasn't purposely trying to keep it a secret, but I don't think we ever talked about my diagnosis. He is a very active man, a curler and skier who does all kinds of sports and has endless energy. I suppose I was holding him back from experiencing the fullness of life that he was used to. He wouldn't contact me over the phone or computer, so I wrote him a letter asking what was wrong and if he had decided to move on and see someone else. He phoned me and said he hadn't, but he thought we should break up. I made arrangements to pick up my things and was able to put them all in my car and finish it all in one trip. He gave me a huge hug and I left with tears pouring from my eyes.

I worked as a case assistant for a year and after that I applied to the R.C.M.P. Victim Services Department to work full-time and to North Battleford Youth Center for a casual call-in position. When I didn't pass my probation at Victim Services, NBYC was glad because I was available to work for them more often. I got more than 40 hours a week there, but my fatigue wouldn't allow me to keep up with the youth during the day. Then a full-time weekend night position became available I applied and since not many people liked working nights, I got it! I would work two or three 12 hour shifts every weekend and also filled in some transporting shifts during the week...until it was decided that a new Mental Health hospital was being built and this one that was housing the youth was going to be shut down.

I decided to apply for work in Lloydminster, an hour from North Battleford and partly in Alberta. Before I left NBYC someone told me not to quit, but to stay on and come in for the odd shift every now and then, so that's what I did. I gave up my full-time job and moved into a basement suite in Kitscoty, 10 minutes out of Lloydminster in Alberta. I worked at Bea Fisher looking after mentally challenged adult First Nation people for a year and smiled every time I would think about being Kelly from Kitscoty!

The money I made there was not too terribly bad, but the conditions in which I had to work were deplorable. They were asking me — with Multiple Sclerosis — to be outside in the dead of winter and shovel snow after a big snowstorm. After that happened I went to see my doctor and she wrote them and told them about my sore back problems. The people I was working with had no experience working with mentally challenged people and I did, so I was making more money than they were and they didn't like that. I did have a master's, but the one First Nations woman working with me had experience being a boss, so they hired her to run the program. She didn't like the fact she was making less money than me and not allowed to work over-time. I would have LOVED to not have to work overtime, and was finished paying child support, so I didn't need the money as much anymore. The other girl had just failed her Licensed Practical Nurse program and was still quite young.

> From this chapter I learned I should have tried talking to my ex instead of taking him to court. He probably told my girls I was doing this and they must have learned to dislike me even more. I hardly heard from my girls and I missed my son and grandchildren like crazy. I also learned that I needed to keep the stress I was feeling while working out of my life, so I did something about it as quickly as I could.

Chapter Eleven

Starting to Polish

THE ACTUAL CLIENTS WHO LIVED at the house where we worked were wonderful people and I would have gone back to work more hours with them, just even to visit. But when an 80% full-time nights position became available at NBYC again, I decided to move back to North Battleford. I applied and was offered the position, but before I agreed to start I asked if I could start the following week because I was scheduled to work that weekend in Lloydminster and they said "No, we need you to start right away." I felt bad for leaving Bea Fisher people to find someone to work that weekend, but my blood pressure went up so very often when I was working there that something had to give. Plus I was living in a basement suite with two guys who worked in the oil field. I didn't see them often because I was usually sleeping when they got home, and off to work before they woke up. That's why the price was so inexpensive.

So I hired some movers to pick my things up in Kitscoty and haul them all back to North Battleford. I even picked up a TV I bought from a friend of mine for $100.00. I loved it, it had a 50-inch screen and it was one of those big heavy ones. I didn't have to carry it, but I did love to watch it! I found another apartment in North Battleford but kept driving back and forth to Regina to visit Corinne and her daughters, then on to Yorkton to visit my parents. About a week or two after I started back full-time at NBYC a weekday nights position became available, I applied and it was offered to me, so I accepted it.

I was back to living in the small town I had grown to love, getting weekends, holidays and E.D.O.s off and was making what I thought was pretty good money. My closest friends were living very far away, in Yorkton, Naniamo, Regina, and my birth family lived in Yorkton, Calgary and Edmonton, so I was quite the distance away from everyone I loved and was close to my heart. I felt lonely and sad, and the depression set in again. One of my new neighbours asked me what the numbers 09/28/00 meant. I told him at one point it was the saddest day of my life, but now I finally realized it was the first day of the BEST of my life!

I did make friends in North Battleford; one woman was a full-time Adult Probation Officer who invited me out with her husband and friends on Wednesday evenings for chicken wings and drinks. I loved her because she was my hero. Diagnosed with cancer when she was eight years old, she went into surgery and woke up when she came out of anesthesia to realize they had taken the bottom half of her leg. She didn't find any prosthetic to be comfortable, so she was always hopping along on her crutches, plus she was dealing with an acquired brain injury from a fall and Diabetes! She would challenge anyone who came into her office saying they couldn't find a job because of some surgery on their leg. She would show them her leg and crutches and let them know she worked 2 jobs so her and her husband could travel on their days off. I also made another friend, a widowed and retired Registered Nurse, who lived on the main floor of the first apartment I had lived at in North Battleford. When we lived in the same building she would always meet me at the front door after work and ask if I wanted to go out to eat and she would offer to buy. I bought dinner for her a few times, but she kept saying I was always driving so she wanted to pitch in somehow, so I stopped offering to buy. She used to have so many interesting stories about her husband who was buried in the graveyard not far from where we lived. I drove her there once to visit his grave. I was wearing slippers at home and didn't change my shoes before I walked out to my car, it was summertime but I didn't want to run up three flights of stairs, so I suggested we grab two to-go coffees and go the graveyard to visit her husband's gravesite.

When I was leaving work one Friday morning and talking about driving to Yorkton to visit my sister, NBYC's Psychologist suggested I eat sunflower seeds to keep my mind occupied and awake for the entire trip and they weren't fattening. I was finally off on weekends and didn't really know anyone in North Battleford and area, so I would travel to Edmonton to wait tables at my Nurse sister's restaurant she bought, or back to Yorkton to visit my sister who also has M.S., or to Regina to spend time with Cori and her girls. I was working weeknights so all week I was usually at home alone.

My parents were upset with me because my mother was sure I had stolen some pictures she was trying to sort so she could clean up their belongings and distribute them to family members. She was busy doing a death cleaning of their home because they had been needing to clean out relative's homes after they died and she didn't want to leave that for her family to do after she died. She was sure I saw the piles of pictures she had accumulated and took one of them, or maybe even some of them and stole them from her room. I hadn't of course, but she didn't believe me. I think I mentioned to someone in front of her too that grandma had accused her of stealing grandma's panties when grandma was Mom's age. Grandma had apologized to her when they were found in a box in the back of her closet where she had forgotten that she had put them.

My daughters were not staying in touch with me either. One weekend my sister Connie called me from Edmonton and said she was driving to Yorkton to visit our parents and she wanted to know if I wanted to go with her. She said she was leaving on a Thursday afternoon and I told her I was working Thursday night until Friday morning and she said she would just drive to North Battleford on Thursday, stop at my place in the evening and sleep in my bed until Friday morning when I got off work, then she would drive us to Yorkton on Friday morning. I said I would go with her as long as she dropped me off at my other sister's place before she continued on to our parent's place. She said she would drop me at the turn-off of the highway to get to my older sister's place, and my older sister said she would pick me up at that corner. I stayed with Karen that weekend, and I think I may have taken the bus back 'home' to North Battleford.

Cori was having trouble in her marriage now too. I thought when I first met him that he was a narcissist and that money and looks were more important to him than Corinne. I didn't say anything to her because my husband was like him, and she married him so she must have loved him, like I loved my husband too when I married him. Cori told me her husband was cheating on her, but he was open and honest about it. She knew the lady and actually liked her, and would be so calm, cool and collected around her, but she was as hurt as I was about my ex and his new wife. It must have hurt her heart as much as my heart would hurt every time I'd see Mark with Suzie, even after they were married. And then Cori found out they were expecting a baby!

So now, my parents were upset with me and I had no idea how to fix that, my brother was in jail, my husband was on his second wife, I was paying for half of both my daughter's post-secondary educations and none of my kids stayed in touch with me at all, and on top of it all, I had MS! It looked like nothing in my life was going to go in my favour, but I still felt bad for Cori. She was doing so well even with her husband having a girlfriend, so I thought maybe I might be able to move to Regina and help her out with her twins and she could help me with my jealousy and depression. Why not? Nobody stayed in touch with me and I couldn't do anything much for anyone either because of my M.S.

I decided to start checking online and in newspapers for apartments and jobs in Regina so I could be nearer to her if and when she needed me. Plus

Regina was only two hours from Yorkton, and not six, like North Battleford was. My brother was in jail in Regina and I would drive there many weekends to visit him and stay with Cori overnight. I attended court with him for his appeal, and there were a couple of guys there I just assumed were his friends, I didn't even recognize my own son. I asked him how he knew my brother and he said "Mom?" My cousin was with me and my tears just poured, but she was very understanding. I offered to buy lunch for everyone and most of us met at East Side Mario's. I toured apartments, interviewed for positions and was finally offered a position at Paul Dojack Youth Center.

PDYC could have been almost like a transfer because I had already been hired to work in a youth jail, so I didn't have to be tested again. The guy who called me up said I just needed to be there to take facility specific training. Plus, they didn't have any full-time nights positions opened. He said when one does come up, if I applied for it, with my seniority I would probably get it. Not many people wanted to work nights in Regina either! And when one did become available, their staff worked rolling shifts, not weekends or weeknights. I would need to work so many in a row, whether it was a weekend or a weeknight. Weekends were 12-hour shifts, and weeknights were nine. I accepted their offer and found a place in the tall apartment building downtown where I had always wanted to live, since the first time I saw it.

I had given my son my phone number and he called me to ask for money. I said that I would, but right now was not a good time because I was having to pay rent at two apartments and pay movers $1800.00 to move me. He said "How much?" I repeated the amount and he said he could move me for half of that one Saturday if I would watch his kids. His kids are my grandchildren so I said of course I would! The mother of his children had the kids taken away for slapping her eldest, who Kyle had been stepfather to since their first son was born. He wanted his kids home and Social Services said "Not if she's in the house," and he said "Fine, she's out!"

He had become a single parent, so he needed some financial assistance from his mother. He found a moving trailer in Regina to rent, and I went to the owner and paid him in advance, so everything Kyle earned from me was cash in his pocket. He asked my foster sister's son to drive them to pick me up and I had to ask Ryan who he was too. I apologized to him and explained my mistake with not recognizing my own son too. He was very understanding and kind. Ryan drove his truck with the trailer behind it, and Kyle rode with him. I drove my car with his children...my grandchildren. I took tons of pictures and thanked Kyle for helping me decide that physician-assisted suicide was not the answer.

I signed up on a dating site again and decided to be open and honest about my MS, but also mention that it hasn't impacted my life as it does for many people. I wanted everyone to know that if they do decide to get together with me that they might need to end up becoming my caregiver, eventually. I kept asking this one guy if he knew what MS was and if he understood that if he got together with me he may end up becoming a caregiver. He said that I wasn't looking for a boyfriend, I was looking for someone to be my caretaker and I was on the wrong site. But most guys were quite understanding and I spent a little time with a few different guys before I decided on one.

> In this chapter of my life I was learning that miracles actually do happen, and maybe Kyle and I were going to start a new chapter together! I loved seeing my grandkids and maybe someday my girls will want to see me again too! If I couldn't find a boyfriend, at least I still had one man (and two boys and one girl) in my life! But...degeneration doesn't stop for anyone or anything.

Chapter Twelve

Polishing Up the Diamond I Was Born to Be

J OHN HAD BEEN MARRIED AND cheated on twice, so divorced twice, but the first evening we went out to drink wine at the piano bar we ate appetizers and kept talking and listening like we had known each other for a million years. That night after he dropped me off at my apartment, he texted me until I fell asleep. I dated a couple more, then decided to stop dating all of them but John. We had met on September 29 and by October 4 I had made up my mind. When I first saw him I didn't think I would ever choose someone with a moustache like his, but I had already decided to not choose anyone ever again for their looks, or lack thereof. John was far from ugly, not as tall as it said he was in his profile, and 12 years older than me, which meant he was older than both my sisters!

We decided to move in together quite early in our relationship, but we both believed he shouldn't have to continue to sleep in his friend's basement anymore. Even though we met after they were officially divorced, most of his things were still in the house he had built for his original family. After the division of property settlement finally went through, we had already put a bid on a house that was fully accessible and close to a guy John knew from a music store he had spent lots of time at. John was not only a Pharmacist, but also a lead guitar player and father of two kids approximately the same ages as my older two.

When our bid was accepted he made arrangements with movers and I made arrangements to pay Kyle to help me move again. Kyle brought his kids with him and his eldest son helped carry the things into the house while I was able to spend time with the younger two. John took us out for dinner that night at a Chinese food place and his son came too, as he was helping his dad at the same time Kyle and his family were helping me. After they went home I cleaned out the apartment and left it cleaner than it was when I moved in.

I decided to switch Neurologists when I read about a newly trained Neurologist opening an MS clinic. I didn't get a call to come in for an M.R.I. for a couple of years, so I called my current Neurologist's office and asked for a referral. I also called my family doctor's office and asked them to send a referral as well. It took three months, but I finally got in and drove the two hours to Saskatoon with John and we both went in to meet Dr. Ilia Poliakov. The doctor introduced himself to us using his first name and John was impressed.

I had known that I wanted to write a book about my life and had started and stopped so many times I lost track. I knew I had done a lot of stuff and had been through so many things that filling up these pages would not be a problem. I was kind of stuck on how to go about it, so I applied for a class at the community college titled Creative Writing. We had to write a story for every class and make it short enough to read in front of the rest of the students in five minutes, so everyone had an equal amount of time to share. I would stand in front of that group and cry every week, but everyone was either a retired teacher or an author, and they were all quite understanding. We even collected a bunch of short stories and put them together in a book that we self-published and named *Write from the Heart*.

Dad had an appointment in Regina with an eye doctor downtown one day, so I said I would meet them for lunch after work. I finished my shift at 8:30 in the morning and his appointment was for 8am. I drove to the hospital where the optometrist's office was and found Mom, Dad and my eldest sister Karen who drove them to Regina. We all went for lunch at Henry's Café where I suggested we eat. My parents were very hungry already as they had eaten breakfast at 5am and it was almost noon. It took the waitress a whole 15 minutes to get our food, but my parents still complained.

A while later, my father's younger brother from Regina died the same morning I went to the hospice to visit him and told my aunts to take a break and go get some lunch. They both had been with him all day and needed to get something to eat, so I said I would stay with Uncle Tony. After they were gone for over half an hour it looked to me like Uncle Tony had stopped breathing. I walked up to the nurse's station and asked if he was hooked up to anything so they would know whether or not he was still alive and they said they would send someone right away to check. A male nurse came in and checked and told me he was gone. I phoned Aunt Fran right away and she said they'd be right there. I asked Uncle Tony to give his mother Angeline a hug from me and say hi to his brother, my Uncle Richard.

The other aunt who was there, Aunt Ollie, is the widow of my Uncle Richard who had passed away suddenly 12 years earlier, so she was there to assist Aunt Fran while sitting at the hospice looking after her dying husband. The nurses thought Aunt Ollie was Aunt Fran's daughter because of the toll Uncle Tony's illness was taking on her. I told Aunt Ollie that I felt bad I had told them to leave when he passed away. Aunt Ollie said not to worry, they were going to go out to eat anyway and he would have been alone. At least he was with family when he passed, and I felt better. We met at Aunt Fran's place that night and drank tea with some whiskey in it.

Dad had an appointment at the general hospital downtown to unblock the 100% blockage in one of his carotid arteries. Mom hadn't mentioned that to me, but Connie called and did. She said Mom told her that if I called and asked her to, they would stay at my place while Dad was in the hospital instead of staying with her nephew who lives in the city. I didn't believe her and I wasn't going to, but in the end, I'm glad I did. Dad had an appointment the day before the surgery in an office downtown, kind of in the middle of the city. They told him to have a bath that night and he said he had bathed the night before so he should be fine. Connie, being a nurse, convinced him and he did have a bath that night. I knew they were coming so I put steak in the slow cooker, potatoes in the oven to bake, and John made sure there was sour cream and bacon bits and everyone had a fine feast the night before Dad's surgery. Mom said she had been craving baked potatoes for a while and she really enjoyed them.

Uncle Tony's funeral was the first and only time in almost six years that John and I went to church together. I no longer attend Catholic mass, and John was raised Lutheran. He was upset with God because of everything he had been through with his second wife, who was Catholic and cheated on him with her first cousin. I still believe in God and Jesus Christ, but not religion. I read the bible every now and then, but I believe that different beliefs in different religions cause war.

Karen and I have stayed close friends and sometimes when she flies in from Naniamo to visit her Mom I will send her a message back and offer to pick her up at the airport and drive her to Yorkton so we can catch up. Her brother David has stopped drinking since their other brother Stephen passed away in his chair at home when he was probably about 52. John and I both drove Karen and David to Yorkton for their father's recent funeral, but we didn't attend. We just visited my parents that day instead.

My sister told me she saw on Facebook that my youngest daughter Angeline was getting married and I was happy for her, even though I wasn't introduced to her husband to be. She sent me a letter to a Facebook account I hadn't used for years and I sent my kids a Happy Halloween text message. Angeline texted me back to ask if I read the letter she wrote to me. I said I hadn't and asked her where she sent it. She told me and I said I haven't checked that account for decades already. I asked her if she would please send it to my new e-mail account and she said she would as soon as she could. She told me she was grateful to me for everything I had taught her but didn't want me at her wedding because of how I made her feel about her father, and the fact that I hadn't paid for her education at the university of Saskatchewan that she didn't even tell me that she was doing. Plus, I didn't help her pay for their wedding, which I knew nothing about. I didn't go, but I did write her back to ask her not to deprive my other family members of her happiness. My parents and eldest sister and her husband went to their wedding and my daughter and her new husband were introduced before their first dance as Dr. and Mrs. Lypka.

I was volunteering at a place where I worked before moving to North Battleford. I kept going to work at night and was offered full-time permanent and I accepted that. The people that worked in the front of the building were always asking me why I was limping when I would come in for work. I would say I didn't realize that I was. We would have a full day of training every 8-12 weeks on a Friday. One of those Fridays in May a team building day was planned. We all met in a hotel conference room and listened to a speaker talk about focusing on the positive 10% of our days and forgetting about the negative 90%. She was great!

Then we went back to the Jail for a barbeque outside and our bosses cooked us hamburgers and hot dogs and their support staff brought in salads and desserts. It was really hot outside so I spent time either staying indoors or sitting in the shade. After lunch we had a tour of the Parliament building downtown where there turned out to be a ton of stairs. I asked the tour guide if there was an elevator and she said there was, but it only fit three people. I didn't want to seem greedy or lazy, so I followed everyone up the stairs. I did have to walk right beside the hand railing and kind of pull myself up with each step. The guy who hired me came to walk beside me, got down low enough to look me in my face and asked me if I was OK. I said "I have to be!" with a smile and kept walking.

The night I went to work after that team building day, my supervisors told me that their boss had asked them to suggest to me that I apply for Long Term Disability. I already had the application and had started filling it out, but now at least I could be assured that my bosses would be in favour. My application was accepted on my first try, as was CPP-Disability (the federal one). Back to volunteering, sleeping in, and taking classes to learn to write my book! I didn't feel sick, in fact I felt I was blessed with M.S. It helped me get out of a marriage that I never should have agreed to in the first place, it didn't take my eyesight, and I hadn't really had a lot of pain that I didn't already have before my diagnosis. I think this past May will be four years since I worked my last day at the jail, and I am finally finishing my book!

L.T.D. and C.P.P. - Disability doesn't pay as much as I was finally getting paid while I was working, and John decided to retire in November 2021 as well, so when I saw an ad for learning how to be a Virtual Coach online, I decided to go for it! I received my Virtual Coaching Certificate from Annie Lala and Eben Pagan after writing my exam in August of 2022. One of the Coaches I met in that class told me I won't die a diamond, I already am one – I was BORN one! I had just been treated like coal for so long that I started treating myself like a piece of coal. I am now taking the *Next Level Course* with Tony Robbins and Dean Graziosi and *Free Sessions that Sell* with Christian Mickelson to polish up my coaching skills before I even get started. I'm also reading a lot of books on coaching, things to do after 50, and abandoned parents. Someday I do hope to reconcile, but I'm not going to let go of my happiness because we don't speak. If I don't let go of my past, I won't be able to enjoy my future. I love all my children, but I need to learn to love them from a distance so I don't allow them to continue to hurt me with their words anymore.

I recently read the *Law of Attraction* by Esther and Jerry Hicks, which talks about thinking only about the positive and not the negative. My brain doesn't understand the word 'not,' so saying I will not be broke, my brain only hears 'be broke.' If anyone ever does anything for me, even fits me in for an appointment on a day I am available to get there I tell them I LOVE them, and sometimes I even say I'll love them forever, with a smile. A smile means the same thing in any language, so if I don't understand what a person is saying, I smile, ask them to say it again, maybe write it down or draw a picture, but I always try to keep that smile on my face.

One time I was walking with Mom around the block I asked her why she gave me a $200.00 cheque last December. She said "For your Birthday and Christmas!" I said yes, but there were six years there when I didn't get anything for my birthday and Christmas because you both felt like I owed you money. She said that was all Dad because he got the cheque back and noticed he had written 'loan' on the cheque and I wasn't making any attempt to repay the loan. When she picks up the phone after I dial their number, I say "Hi there beautiful!" or "Hello Gorgeous!" She says she thinks I dialed the wrong number, but I ask if this is (her name) and she says "Yes, but I'm not Beautiful." I tell her she is on the inside, but she says she doesn't agree with me.

I even started saying "I love you' before hanging up the phone after talking with my parents, and Dad says "I love you" every time he says goodbye and Mom is starting to as well! After I had been texting with Connie for quite some time, she told Mother that I was bedridden so when we walked into her house the next time she was overjoyed, but upset with Connie. I told her that by my words it probably did sound worse than it was. Mom said she wanted to come to Regina but wasn't sure how they could. I told her not to worry about it, and that if or when I do become bedridden, a phone call would be enough to make me feel better.

> I've learned to laugh, live, love, learn, forgive and forget, but some of these lessons were easier to learn than others. I've lived quite a full life, I'm glad I got an education after dropping out the day I turned 16. I'm also glad I may be able to convince my parents that saying I love you is not such a bad thing after all. I hope to someday reconcile with my children because I know how horrible they will feel if I die before they realized that I really did love them all more than life itself. For the first couple of years I would write Angeline a letter on her wedding anniversary, so I've copied and pasted the final letter I wrote to my youngest daughter three years after her wedding. I don't always know how to show it, but I have and will love all of my children and grandchildren forever. Because I love them so very much and always have, I can't imagine living the rest of my life without them. However, I have accepted the fact that if I have to, I will continue loving the memory of them.

My Final Letter

Dear Mrs. Angeline Lypka,

THIS WILL BE THE FINAL letter I write to you, unless and until at some point you feel merit in responding respectfully. That doesn't mean I will ever stop loving and thinking of you constantly. I do, however, need to guard my own self-respect and my feelings which have merit too. All of my children have decided to stay away from me because of the way you feel I've treated you. I now need to guard my feelings and resolve that I was treated harshly and unfairly as well.

Your father and I were both immature and unhealthy when we separated, and I wish we both would have been able to treat each other with respect, for the sake of our children. Today I would never even consider comparing the maturity between your father and me. I didn't ever think I would be able to fall in love again either because of everything your father and I went through. But even though John has been married before he and I love each other and wish to spend the rest of our lives together. We just want to be together, leaning on each other, and supporting each other as best we can. I am hoping that one day I could have a respectful and cordial relationship with your father and his wife and family for the sake of our children, as I have with John's children.

Some really mean things about your father were said, and I do apologize, again. If we had been able to even maintain a cordial relationship for the sake of our children, I probably would have been invited to your wedding. I might have been told you were continuing your education in Saskatoon, and given the chance to pay for half, or at least a part of it. Your grandfather bought some land while you were still quite young and said the proceeds from the rent of that land would be put towards his granddaughters' future education. I probably would have been included in your wedding plans. I would have even figured out a way to contribute towards that post-secondary education and towards your wedding expenses. My parents paid to raise 4 children plus foster children, so they never had the resources your father was raised with, being an only child, but they did the best they could.

I wish your father and I could have been more respectful towards each other when we separated which would have contributed to being better role-models to the children we both brought into this world. I didn't ask him to pay alimony, which I could have because of my diagnosis. Plus I did pay child support in full, which I have a letter from the government to prove that I did. His lawyer included all kinds of new and expensive things he bought for you that I wouldn't have been able to afford, but I figured out a way to pay for half. I did pay for half of your original post-secondary education even though I was never once included in any conversation regarding the post-secondary education of either one of our girls. He did not include how much money his father was helping you out with, so I did pay more than my fair share.

Let me be clear, my love for you is unconditional, but your presence in my life is not mandatory. The moment you decided to leave me out of one of the most important days in your life you showed how little you think of me. I find that I need to protect my sense of self-worth, I had and still have no problem unconditionally loving the memory of you. Because if I don't let the past die, it won't let me live.

There are a lot of people in my life now who do want to see me and spend time with me-the family of my heart. They include us in their Christmas plans, celebrate our birthdays, allow us to celebrate theirs with them, and basically treat us like family. They also understand the regret I have in being a part of raising children who value money more than me in their life. We do now finally realize what it's like to be financially comfortable rather than strapped every day as I felt for many years, thanks to the education I got which I paid for all by myself.

How glad you must be that you were married before the pandemic hit! I still wish I could have been there and I was, in my heart. I hope and pray you and your husband both always have and will continue to treat each other with complete respect for the rest of your lives. I really and truly look forward to hearing from you as soon as you feel comfortable speaking with me.

Love always and in all ways,

Your mom

About The Author

KELLY HAS BEEN MEDICALLY RETIRED since 2019, lives with her retired Common-Law Husband John in Regina, the capital city of Saskatchewan, Canada. She is ready, willing and able to apologize and reconnect with all three of the human beings she helped bring into this world. Until then, she loves to write, read, watch 'Criminal Minds' and 'Friends' reruns and the same movies over and over. She also has a passion for helping others get through the same kinds of things she's been through. Her home-based Virtual Coaching Business can be reached at SparkleLikeADiamond.ca.

Kelly can also be reached for speaking engagements at (639) 590-5500 or by email at StankewichKelly@gmail.com

Testimonials

"I loved reading Kelly's life story. It's beautiful and truly touched my heart. I admire her strength and her perseverance, despite all obstacles she encountered in her life. Her courage to take responsibility for her life is remarkable.

I admire Kelly for pursuing her education and personal growth, she is a proof that everything is possible, if you really want it.

She inspired me to be brave to go through the process of writing my own story, even if it's painful.

You truly are a sparkling diamond Kelly. "

Eva Vecchio, artist and coach, Italy

Kelly's Courageous storytelling is one of perseverance through life's obstacles. She shows that labels or diagnosis don't confine who you are and that healing the outside starts from healing within........

Gigi Damle, Psychologist and Coach, USA

One afternoon, I had the rare opportunity to have this shero's journey read to me by the author herself. Kelly is a resilient woman who is inspiring others by sharing her story. Enjoy!

**Jade Mahon
Life Coach, Canada**

"Searching For My Sparkle" At first read the characters immediately Came alive, causing me to Live in the moment and be absorbed in their energy, strength , love and pain. I was completely overtaken with anticipation to read more.

Maria Flores-Sperling PhD, CAC-II
Mental health, substance disorder,
HIV /AIDs counselor
Georgia, USA

Reflections

_____

_____

_____

_____

_____

Searching For My Sparkle

Reflections

www.ingramcontent.com/pod-product-compliance
Lightning Source LLC
Chambersburg PA
CBHW041308110526
44590CB00028B/4283